a collection of relatable thoughts

To Catalina's Mum.

I am so glad you gave
me a friend. Thank you
for being an awesome mum,
I hope you enjoy
this book.
                    love
                    Evergreen
                    (23-11-19).

a collection of relatable thoughts

Everlyne Nyambura

Matador
9 Priory Business Park,
Wistow Road, Kibworth Beauchamp,
Leicestershire. LE8 0RX
Tel: 0116 279 2299
Email: books@troubador.co.uk
Web: www.troubador.co.uk/matador
Twitter: @matadorbooks

ISBN 978 183859 155 7

British Library Cataloguing in Publication Data.
A catalogue record for this book is available from the British Library.

Printed and bound in the UK by TJ International, Padstow, Cornwall
Typeset in 10pt Sabon by Troubador Publishing Ltd, Leicester, UK

Matador is an imprint of Troubador Publishing Ltd

Writing my first book has been a rollercoaster. I want to thank God for being with me on this ride and being my strength.

Thank you to my friends and family for supporting me and encouraging me every time I wanted to give up.

To the publishing team at Matador, thank you for guiding me through this self publishing journey, for your kindness and patience. And for giving me the opportunity to share my words with the world.

To my connect group, you guys are special and hold a place in my heart. I love you all.

And to Catalina Marin. I cherish our friendship. Thank you for walking this path with me. You are a talented artist and I'm lucky to have you in my life.

Contents

Introduction

A Collection of Relatable Thoughts is a book full of poetry, letters, and encouraging conversations that dives into the realities of life. Its aim is to encourage you the reader to reflect on your everyday thoughts and life experiences, and to motivate you to make better choices daily. The feelings expressed in this book are universal. We're not going through them alone, there are others who share your feelings. Our situations may be different, but we all pretty much have similar thoughts along our journeys. The truth is, we're all connected together through our pain and vulnerabilities. But we are not destined to stay there, we should help each other break free and move on to a healthier future.

The book is broken into five chapters with each one exploring a different mindset:

1. Battleground; looks at how overpowering negative thoughts can be when we are feeling defeated.
2. Them vs You; the detrimental impact of comparing ourselves to others.
3. Relationship; the way that our relationships shape different parts of us.
4. Learning Curve; becoming your most authentic self through a journey of self-discovery.
5. Soaring; being your best self.

Along with the entries, there are a few simple activities to guide you on different ways you could improve your own life; I encourage you to take some time going through these. Each chapter has a suggestive activity and a mindful colouring activity.

Life happens now. And whether you like it or not, you can't postpone being in the moment. I started doing mindful colouring to pass time during my night shifts when I worked in a mental hospital. It was something that I did to keep myself awake. But I started to find it more therapeutic when I was feeling anxious and I needed something to help me chill out. If you're dealing with more serious mental issues, mindful colouring alone won't be as effective, so you should also consider seeking further professional help.

Sometimes we get caught up in worrying about what's next, or what will happen tomorrow. The mindful colouring activities are meant to encourage you to rein in your wandering mind back to focus on the present moment. As you do them, don't worry if your mind roams elsewhere. Let it wander, but just lead it back to the task. The reason I decided to include this activity is to expose the people around me to a different way of dealing with stress. Try it out, and then decide for yourself whether it is something you may want to continue doing in the future.

The suggestive activities offer alternative activities that you can try to reduce stress, build connections or to help you set goals in the future. Try the ones that you haven't before and see if they add any positive change to your life.

You are also expected to read this book in order from the first chapter to the last, so that you are able to see the progression of thoughts through the chapters. Every entry is listed on the content page, so if you have a certain thought that is mentioned in this book it is easy for you to flick back and re-read.

I would like to share my experiences with you to show you, that you are not alone. So one day you may share your stories too, they are what connects us to each other.

I hope you enjoy reading this as much as I enjoyed writing it and find encouragement within these pages.

Everlyne Nyambura
September 2019

battle ground

deep breaths

It doesn't have to be epic.
Just do what comes naturally.
Breathe child.

Don't overthink about the outcome.
Just focus on this moment.
This moment won't come again, so take it all in.
Breathe child.

Let's try a grounding exercise.
Deep breaths.
How are you feeling right now?
Inhale, exhale.
What are you doing right now?
Inhale, exhale.
What can you see around you?
Inhale, exhale.
What's the weather like outside?
Inhale, exhale.
Sit by the window, open it and take a deep breath.

How do you feel now?

overthinking

Maybe it's not as hard as what I make it to be

Maybe cos I expect it to be hard, I make it harder for myself

Creating silly reasons as to why I'm going to fail

My mind mixes up the words challenging and impossible

> I overthink situations that are unlikely to happen, and they seem real to me

Instead of focusing on writing, I spend my days creating a horror movie in my mind

> I end up killing my creativity with all of my unrealistic expectations and exaggerated thoughts
> Then call myself useless when I can't produce anything

And sometimes my creativity triggers my anxiety

Cos I'm overthinking the end product

> I want it to be perfect

sorry

I'm disappointed in myself today
    I did what I said I would stop doing
I lost self-control
And blew everything out of proportion

I lied to myself again
    Sorry Eve

Please forgive me

frustrated

It seems like everyone around me knows what they want
They all march towards something
With ambition

As I lay in bed
Waiting for the wind to speak to me
Anything
Waiting for the universe to tell me what I need to do

Stagnant days turn into weeks

Frustrated at those who have a five-year plan
I barely have a one-month plan

My mind is so childlike
Easily distracted by what looks good
Inconsistent like a child who cries for ice-cream, but wants
cake when they see someone else eating cake

Frustrated that I can't hop out of bed
 Get myself ready
 And do what I was born to do

Instead, I get to watch others do what they were born to do
 They look so happy
Whilst I continue to lay in bed trying to figure it all out

Looking back, I was where I needed to be
I needed to experience the lows first
It's what made me who I am today

You'll understand that too someday

prisoner

The keys are dangling off the exit door
Begging me to make a run for it
But a giant shadow lingers
My secrets stand tall, guarding the door
Ready to expose me if I try to escape

I'm being kept hostage by guilt
A prisoner of shame
So I turn my back to the door
Hopeless
And gaze out the window longing for freedom
Rotting alone in the cell

What's wrong with me?
The keys are right there
I thought I wanted to be free

So, I start planning my escape route
How can I get out of here without being hurt?
How can I get out of here without being exposed?

I don't want anyone to know that I was ever locked up

But the only way out comes with a battle
Having to come face to face with my insecurities and shame

It's the cost of freedom

Today will not be that day
I'm weak in spirit
I'll stay locked in for one more night
I'm not ready to fight

Maybe tomorrow I'll be ready

But this is all on me
I'm the one refusing to open the cage
I'm the captor

battleground

I have an angel and a demon both whispering in my ear
My mind is their boxing ring
And they fight all the time

I'm really rooting for the angel
She's gentle yet fierce
She makes me feel safe
Her kind words save my soul
I love it when she wins
She makes me feel unstoppable
She makes me feel loved

And then there's the demon
She condemns
She shames

It's a dark place when she wins

isolation

Loneliness tells me to isolate myself, so you don't feel
sorry for me
I don't want your pity
I don't want you to see me like this
It's embarrassing
My instinct is to withdraw
Allowing myself to go doormat
Feeling fragile

Just leave me the tools to fight on your way out
And when I'm ready I'll come to you and we'll fight together

But until then, leave me alone

lost voice

I wasn't able to handle change
And in the end, I lost my voice
It felt like no one was listening anyway

But people noticed
So I blamed it on being a shy and quiet person

I wasn't always shy
But the more I blamed being shy
The more I became it
And slowly I started to limit myself
Doubting everything I did
Life slowly withdrew from me

Every conversation ending with a "you used to be so…"
Ah
Stop reminding me

I don't laugh the way I used to
I don't have that confidence I used to have
I don't have that peace I used to have

The hope I used to cling on to, vanished

I wanted to be the girl I used to be
I miss the old me

Can I ever go back to the person who I was before?

Is she lost forever?

She was so carefree
She was happy
She enjoyed her life

Do you ever miss the old version of yourself?

too much effort

The thought of being in a room with other people makes
me uncomfortable

They are not just random people
They are my friends, my people

They didn't do anything wrong to me
It's not their fault

It's just too much effort to hold a conversation

Too much effort to bring out 'lively Eve' tonight
Having to draw a smile on my face and carry it all night

Meanwhile, behind the smile
The truth of loneliness weighs down my soul

Nah
I would rather be alone

This is all too heavy for me

wandering

Torn about which path to take
Making mistakes
Tripping over myself

Led by insecurities
Not knowing my place in the world
Following paths that people tell me to take

Feeling off course
Like I'm not the captain of my life
Not the one sailing the boat
But being bullied by the wind to move wherever it forces
me to go

I'm still young, yet feel like I haven't done enough
Feeling like I've wasted time in my life
That I should be doing more

Instead all I'm doing is wandering
Scrambling in all directions
Trying to fulfil the emptiness inside

What is your purpose?

If only someone told me that when you follow your heart
Whatever direction you take, it will lead you to your true
treasure

the voice that you listen to

When I read out loud
    I notice my voice
    I hear a nobody
    A regular tea biscuit

    It sounds so casual
    So basic

Who would want to listen to me?
    I don't even want to listen to myself

The words are pretty, but I made them sound so dull
    My art started to sound dull to me
    I wanted others to read my work with the sound of life
    flowing through their voices

    The voice I was listening to was not the one coming out
    my mouth
    But the one in my head
    The loudest voice

It told me this is a waste of my time
    I listened
    It told me no one cared
    I listened
    It told me I was ridiculous
    I listened

I try to quieten that voice
    But sometimes it pushes through into a microphone

Sometimes I hear another voice
    I try to listen to it
    It's the voice that cheers me on
    "You're capable, important, needed."
    The voice that tells me "One day at a time."
    The voice that makes me trust myself again

    The voice that gives me hope

    Which voice are you listening to today?

self-handicapping

Dear Eve,

Hope you're okay; last week you said something strange about yourself and I was wondering whether you realised that you take pleasure in self-handicapping a lot these days? Is everything okay?

Do you know what I mean by self-handicapping?

Self-handicapping is something that people do to protect their self-esteem from potential failure. It's something that we all do. Some more than others, but I'm sure we have all done it at some point.

Let me give you an example of two ways people do this:

a. Creating obstacles: making things harder for themselves so that, if they fail it was out of their control.
b. Reducing their efforts: Some people don't like to show others how much effort they put into things. There is nothing worse than giving it your all to have it be unsuccessful. It hurts more especially if there's an audience to witness it.

The problem with this behaviour is that it often places blame on something or someone else when things go pear-shaped. You're most likely to do this when you are unsure about your own ability. No one likes to think of themselves as a failure, but is that how you're feeling these days?

I'm sure you're not doing it on purpose. We don't exactly walk around saying "Let me protect my self-esteem". It kind of just happens automatically and not everyone has the self-awareness to notice when they are doing it. I don't blame you. Some people are so conditioned to believing that succeeding is out of their reach, so they hold their 'reasons' at the tip of their tongues ready to prove to others why they may fail.

And their excuses become the reasons as to why they shouldn't step out of the box and try.

Have you ever heard an excuse literally coming out of your mouth? And you think to yourself "Wow I'm actually making up excuses." Yeah those are the moments to be aware of, so you can quickly change your thoughts to fight those excuses.

Your excuses can become your reality.

I personally think we speak things into existence, so if you walk around preparing to fail, chances are, you probably will.

Don't sell yourself short because you think you might fail honey.

Self-handicapping becomes a problem when you constantly participate in this behaviour and I've noticed this about you recently, Eve. I want the best for you. Sure, making excuses helps you feel better for now, but when you hinder your performance for whatever reason, you are stalling and not giving yourself the best chance.

So, stop tripping and maximise your potential girl!

the anger cycle

It's exhausting
I don't want to embody the 'Angry Black Woman' stereotype
But every day I live it

It's exhausting
Angry at people who fail me
Angry at people who abandon me
Angry at myself for letting it get to me

It wears me out

It feels like I have a weighted cloak wrapped around my body
And every time I try to pull it away someone is wrapping it
even tighter

I can't breathe

I don't want to keep this energy anymore
It's hard work
Something has to change
I just want to experience peace
Oh, how it must be nice

blindfolded

Sometimes I feel so lost
But you're with me, so I can't be lost.

I don't know where I'm going
Trying to navigate through life with slow steps
My arms stretched out, feeling my way around unknown
obstacles

I can't see where I'm going, but You can
And I'm trusting You to lead me

destructive

Today was a close call
I was so tempted
I even let myself imagine just a little

Then I remembered I'm meant to be fighting this
But I still closed my eyes
It tells me I need it
I know it will feel good
It always does
For a while

That thing that shifts your focus
The thing that you love and hate

What was innocent at first took over
It's the only part of my life that I don't have control over

I can go days, weeks without it
But all it takes is just the one thought
A magnetic force pulls me back
Then all my hard work is gone

Out of sight, out of mind
Should I indulge, one last time and that will be the end
Then say a prayer later?
He knows I am trying

I've given God certain areas of my life
And hidden the rest
Especially this one

Every time I think I'm over it, it comes back harder
Is it a curse?

I keep on doing the things I know I shouldn't do
A recurring theme that needs to be broken

My paralysis
Bondage
Strongholds in my mind

A slavery mentality that hungers for the forbidden fruit that
doesn't keep me satisfied

I need to give all of my struggles to God
So that they can no longer hold me captive

Something needs to happen
I have to equip myself for the battle that is yet to come
I can't give up

What is holding you back?

Activity: Mindful Colouring

What is your forbidden fruit?

switching lanes

Have you ever been stuck in a queue?
And the queue next to you seems to be moving faster
So you switch lanes
Then suddenly the queue you were first on starts to move quicker
But now you've lost your spot
And the queue you're now in seems to have slowed down

If only you had a little more patience

Now you have to decide whether you want to go back to the
first queue and start again or stay where you are even though
things are moving slower now
Confused as to what queue to stand in
Impatient to get to the front

And we do this with our lives too
In our quest to be successful
We keep switching lanes
Trying to look successful ahead of our time

Watching other people thrive and accelerate
And we want that too
So we switch to their lane
Trying to keep up
But the road ahead of us is foggy
We can't see where we are going

And we find ourselves stuck at a red traffic light

This was me when I was unemployed
Instead of focusing on one thing, I was just hopping about
trying to make it look like I've still got things going
Instead of waiting and riding out the fast and slow moments
life has to offer
In reality, my inconsistency was what pushed me further back

That's what it looks like when you try to take shortcuts to
your destination

overwhelmed

Feeling overwhelmed today.
Things are starting to pile up on top of me.
Money problems.
Work problems.
Eve problems.
Not motivated to solve any of them.
I stayed in bed all day today, and yesterday too.

My safe place became my trigger.
Robbed of my peace.
What would you ask for if you had a genie?
I would ask for a clear head.
Clarity.

Fighting back tears cos I don't want to answer anyone's questions.
The back of my throat is so tense.
My nose stings.

Life is such a rollercoaster.

After a few circular loops, I feel so dizzy and nauseous that I can't enjoy being on the straight track for a while.
Strong motion sickness even after I've gotten off the ride makes me regret getting on the it in the first place.

Activity
Pick-me-up-list

Feel overwhelmed? Worn out? Stressed?

Everyone has different things that triggers stress. Below, I have noted a few ways that could help someone to manage their stresses and worries. Have a look and see if there are any that you could potentially start doing.

- **Accept** that life serves stress out to everyone at some point in their lives. Life's not a linear road and has ups and downs. Be aware that you will have good seasons and not so good seasons.
- **Do something nice for yourself.** I would like to say every day, but sometimes we can get busy so a minimum of once a week.
- **Log out of social media for a few days of the week.** Just being away from it all can be so refreshing.
- **Exercise at least twice in a week.** Even if you can manage a ten minute walk every day, you'll start to feel the difference mentally and physically. Go running in the park. Go to the gym. Dance. Just get moving.
- **Have dinner with friends/loved ones.** I make it my mission to dine with my friends/family regularly; interaction with loved ones brings so much peace.
- **Finish that book you keep putting down.** I had this one book that took me over a year to finish; I just didn't make time for it. It wasn't even boring, I was just being lazy, I

guess. Whenever I picked up a book there was always a better option to do in my free time (*cough* watch shows).

- **Create something.** Use your imagination. Start a new project. Draw. Write a song. Re-vamp your room or something.
- **Listen to at least one podcast a day.** I'm sure you can spare an hour. On the bus or on your lunch break. These will keep you motivated, and I tend to listen to them the most on my low days.
- **Reach out.** Talk to someone you trust.
- **Journaling.** If you prefer to write rather than talk then express your thoughts and feelings in a private journal/diary.
- **Soak your feet in warm water.** Let me tell you, I feel so good when I soak my feet after a long day, with some nice smelling candles/incense sticks.
- **Pray.** Empty whatever is burdening your heart. Talk to the being who is greater than you.
- **Manage your time.** Get organised, I use the 'Notes' and 'Calendar' apps so much now; that's where I keep my to-do list and other things. Plan and set goals. Start doing things about thirty minutes earlier than you should.
- **Massage.** Now, this is relaxing. You could go to a salon or have someone that you know do it. Loosen up those tight knots.
- **Pamper yourself.** Don't just wait for your birthday. Face masks, haircuts, shopping; whatever satisfies you.
- **TV.** Follow a TV series to temporarily distract yourself if you are feeling highly distressed. I would suggest a few hours of watching something then trying to deal with the source of the stressor after cooling down.

- **Dealing with the source.** Avoiding it won't make it go away. Try writing down what is stressing you. Try out different coping methods. Research ways to address the stressors.
- **Cry.** A good old cry makes me feel better for a while. Just let yourself cry if you need to.
- **Sleep.** Take some rest. Some people have even more difficulty going to sleep when they are stressed. Some methods to help you fall asleep include not having your phone/screens prior to bed. Meditate instead, with deep breathing to relax your body. Try having herbal teas, or sip on some hot water. And relax your body with a hot bath prior to bed.

fractured

For a long time, I felt broken
Not sure what caused the fracture
But always felt anxious inside
Something wasn't right

I wanted to be who people thought I was
I admired that person too
But I also wanted them to know who I really was

I have to live with both versions of myself
But you only see one

Yes I can be lively
I can spend the whole day laughing with you
Then go home a different person
Feeling displaced

Do you only have one version of yourself?
Is that normal or am I making it up?

cycle

It feels like all I do is never enough
No matter what

Overwhelmed by my lack

And now I'm in a cycle
Continuous making bad decisions
Sugar coating my situations because deep down I don't know
what I'm doing

I just always end up picking the wrong options
No matter what

me, myself, and I

Self-pity makes me feel good.
She takes care of me.
And wraps me up like a mother does to her child on a cold day.

I can always count on her to always be there to soothe me.
And remind me that no one really cares.

"Why are you always the first one?" She asks.
"To message people."
"To make sure they are okay."
She then whispers lies to me, that my efforts are not reciprocated.

Left feeling like I'm not enough.
Wallowing in self-pity.

So I pull myself away from everyone.
It's been a hard road.
And She tells me it's better to sit alone.
Because if I'm alone, then there's no one to hurt me.
And I'll have no expectations.
Which makes sense, right?

"It's not by force." She says.
"You don't need their company."

Yes

I don't need anyone anyway
As long as I have Jesus by my side
I don't need them

She smiles "That's right, you don't need them."
"You have me."

Sometimes I feel like it's just easier to be alone
Just me, myself, and I

transparent

All this honesty is killing me
> Allowing myself to be transparent
> Letting everyone know what really goes on in my mind

> There are different ways for me to escape

> By being in denial
> By distracting myself with work
> Drugs and alcohol
> Or Isolating myself

> But I won't do any of those
> I'll write, pray and love myself a little bit more

> But if this will help someone else
> Then I'm willing to wake up every day and bring more
> of myself to them

outbursts

Day 1
"I need to change this."

Day 20
"Arrrrrghhhh stupid me."

Day 36
"What's wrong with me?!!!!!"

Day 54
"I give up."

Day 70
"Let's start again."

loading

Is there a magic fix?
Can someone tell me the secret?

I want to wake up and feel whole
Not wake up every day feeling incomplete

As if I'm still downloading
Not 100 per cent

Can someone tell me what I need to do?

I'm getting impatient
What am I missing?

bottom tier

The last one
The last one
The last one

The undeserving one
Always coming up short
Never good enough

The outcast
The less than

I don't get it
What am I not doing right?

What do I need to do?

your presence

I'm told that You're always with me
And I'm trying my best to believe that

But I can't feel You
I'm so alone

Where are You?

I need You

public speaking

When I'm asked to speak in front of people:

I s-s-stutter
    My voice s h a k e s
    I mispronounce everything
    My mind shuts down
    I become breathless from fear
    The pressure of sounding perfect weighs down on me

    Then I feel dumb for even trying

it's my pain

I hate it when people underestimate my pain and my struggles

Would you like to see me dip my toes in lava?
     (Okay, that's dramatic)
Then will my pain be justifiable to you?

Or should I cut off my limbs?
     (Still dramatic)
How far should I take it in order to satisfy your definition of pain?

     Why is it that your problems are real problems, but my problems are nothing?
     Yes. We're going through different things, but

I can handle only what I can handle
I'm allowed to feel the way I do
     These feelings are real
     And I can't just shut them out because you said so

So don't tell me what's painful to me

God's voice – part 1

"Call to me and I will answer you and tell you great and unsearchable things you do not know." Jeremiah 33:3 (NIV)

You're with company.
Someone is speaking about the day they heard God's voice clearly speak to them.
But you can't help but think He must be ignoring you.
Why does it seem like God speaks to everyone else but me?
The amount of times you've waited to hear his voice.
Maybe you have but you didn't realise who was speaking?

I don't know what to expect.
A deep sound?
I'm struggling with envy for people who can hear His voice with clarity.

"Meditate on his word and surely you'll hear from him" they say.
So I do.
And wait to unlock a new level of 'Christianess'
I close the Bible and sit on my bed.

Nothing.

Let me get on my knees.
Nothing again.

This is so confusing to me and it makes me feel like I'm failing at this Christian thing.

But that doesn't sit right in my heart.

Maybe my heart's not in the right standing.

I know I'm looking at other people's relationships with God and comparing myself.

I think I've fallen so far away.

This isn't what I want.

I've got a lot of growth to do.

hope

I'm all for hope.

It guides you at your weakest point and motivates you to endure difficult times.

Giving you a yearning to live and an openness to new experiences.

A sense of possibility.

The presence of hope draws out a person's strengths, purpose and meaning of life.

An anticipation of something that is yet to be.

For me, being hopeful helps me overcome uncertainty and inspires me not to give up.

But I must admit, sometimes I take it too far.

My hope sometimes starts to create an illusion of a better tomorrow.

Leaving me stuck and avoiding reality.

Sometimes we have unrealistic expectations and can turn the beauty of hope into something sour.

Wishful thinking.

For example, when something is important to you and you hope that it will become yours.

Even though your chances are low, you refuse to acknowledge the reality of your expectations.

A person. A job. An opportunity.

There's a fifty per cent chance. But we choose to ignore the other fifty per cent.

You've gotten caught up in the excitement of this 'opportunity'

that you've given yourself.
Even started making adjustments to your own life.
Feeding your fantasy.
You're so far gone you've forgotten that a coin can land on
either side.
It's a fool's paradise.
This story can only end in two ways.
Heads: congratulations
Tails: unfortunately

Hope can become mistaken with denial if you're not careful.
I personally think that hopefulness is a process that needs a
person to not just wait on good luck to fall at their feet but
have realistic expectations and be prepared for disasters.

Be mindful my loves.
Yes, let's stay positive, but remember that anything is possible.

two worlds within

What do you do when?

You are moving forward in one area of your life
But being held back in another?

When you're a winner in one world
And a loser in the other?

You don't know if you should be celebrating or mourning?

When you're sometimes righteous, and sometimes petty?

When you have two different images of yourself?

When you want to love but you're full of anger?

Stuck in a place of conflict
Competing voices in your head creating so much noise

What do you do?

Firstly, I'm sorry you're feeling this way

But here's what you do

You fix your eyes above

And He will fix you

I've got myself

Right now, the only thing I've got
Are my own words of encouragement

And it's really painful
To have a positive attitude about myself
Especially when doubt torments my mind
To keep supporting myself when every thought tells me
to stop trying
That I'm not going to amount to anything
I've let bad thoughts intimidate me

The enemy has been feeding me with lies
And I've stood there
Defenceless
Letting his arrows pierce through me

How sweetly other people describe you doesn't matter if
you don't believe those kind words about yourself to be true.

I blindly have to trust myself
Speak blessings to myself even when I don't believe it
Because I'm all I've got
And if you can't encourage yourself, do you expect others
to encourage you?

I've got to unlock this mind if I want to achieve things
And you have to do the same too
Be gentle to yourself
Sometimes it will feel like you're the only one cheering for
yourself

may the odds be with you

I'm trying to defy the odds
In a world that can sometimes be a horrible place
Because people lost the ability to believe in themselves
So they want to take you down with them

You just want to set yourself apart
And make an impact

But you feel so small
Up against the whole world

How can I encourage them to believe in themselves
When I can't even believe in myself

me too

People like me
The all-rounders
We just get on with things
It looks like we don't have any struggles
And things just come easy to us
Running on cruise control

So, when life takes a left turn
People find it hard to believe

Because everyone looks at you as if you have your life in order
And it makes you feel like you're not allowed to hurt

So then you water down how you feel
And tell yourself you're not suffering as much as other people

Disregarding your own feelings
But knowing that something's not right

The longer I dismissed it, the worse I got
A war raging within me

If people knew I was struggling they wouldn't lean on me for support
And I was trying to be that person that gives everyone else hope
But you can't give what you don't own

A superhero complex
Taking on everyone's burden
Giving myself responsibilities that I didn't need to
And giving myself unnecessary pressure

But I'm only human

To everyone, it seemed like I was one of those lucky people
You know, the ones that cruise by life

They can only see Superman
Forgetting that Clark Kent lives beneath the costume

But life doesn't play favourites
And it broke me

I came to realise that so many people just like me put on a
brave face

And let me tell you
Pretending is exhausting

So I stopped and opened up to a few people

And now to you

Because this makes healing easier

Then there's a real potential of things getting better
the only question I've got

God, how can I be most effective in this world?
Who do you need me to be?

them vs you

Social MEdia

Me me me
That's what we've come to

Focused on ourselves all the time
Always offended because we make everything about us

The screens have become our gateway for comparison
Opening the door to suffocation with a click of a finger

Watching others enjoy life more than you
Comparing your off-screen life with their story highlights
Then punishing yourself for not living up to their demands

It's not necessarily fake, just not the whole story
An illusion created that suggests a perfect life

A platform made for simple interactions turned into a punishing chamber
That's the dark side of social media

Struggling to keep up in this fast paced, dramatically evolving society we live in
Trying to prove that we're still valuable
That we are the ones to watch
That they are the ones missing out

FOMO

I am missing out
I want to be involved

We look at what they are doing, and it looks better or more
important than what we are doing

You want what they have
And truth be told, they want what you have

Our identities clouded with people's expectations
Trying to become someone who you were never meant to be
Then wondering, "Why do they get it all?"

You're never fully content
Never fully satisfied with what you have

They say the eyes are the windows to our souls
So we must be careful with what we expose ourselves to

It's okay to enjoy and congratulate people online
Nothing wrong with that
But just don't let it make you feel bad about your own life

Don't let unrealistic expectations of others determine how you
choose to live your life
Crazy to say, but they may not even be living up to their own
expectations

potential

Why is it that you see the best in others?
But not in yourself?

You shy away from volunteering yourself
Count yourself out
But you're quick to nominate the ones that you think are
better than you

You're just as good
Everybody knows it but you

You don't see the potential that you have
There's so much you can do
So much talent that you hide and waste

And I wish you could just see yourself differently

I am tired of you second guessing yourself
I am tired of you counting yourself out
You need to leave your old mentality behind

We need you to be ready to step up
To be that great person that you've always wanted to be

I see a powerful person in your future
I see a great leader and encourager that the world needs

Every step that you decide to take, leads us to that person

There's a shift coming your way
I can feel it

rehearsals

We are drawn to people who are experts at what they do
Everything they do is perfect
They make it look so effortless

We admire and wish we were more like them

But behind the scenes they have put months, maybe years of
    practice into their craft
They've had moments when they thought of throwing it all
    away
They've had times when they wished they hadn't started it in
    the first place
But we only ever see the results
We only see their trophies

Then we go and apply pressure on ourselves to succeed
And become frustrated when things don't work out quickly

You want to be great too
But you're not prepared for the process
You tell yourself to enjoy this journey, but you still wish you
    could fast-forward the process

It's all about patience and endurance while you work with
    what you have for the time being
Your trial periods
This is where you discover more of yourself

The time when you can work on your character
Sharpen who you are
Unfortunately, this part can't be skipped
You need to be in the water to learn how to swim

Not everything will come to you at one time
There are some things that you can only learn through
    experience
And you have to keep showing up to the rehearsals

A child must first crawl before they can walk
And in that time, they are eagerly watching as everyone else
    around them walks with ease
But, in due time, they will be walking and eventually running

So we have to master the basics before moving on to the next
    level

pick 'n' mix

We are all different
We bring different items to the picnic
We should embrace that
We shouldn't be ashamed of being different
You're a masterpiece the way you are

The fact that we are all different is a blessing
Imagine going to a party to find that everyone came with only pears?
Where is the variety?
Borringgg

I bet you would be disappointed

When people try to mould themselves to fit the status quo it's like
An orange wearing a pear costume
A banana wearing a pear costume
Or a strawberry wearing a pear costume

None were designed to be pear shaped
And they can never be a pear

I have nothing against pears
But I want a fruit salad type of lifestyle
If everyone chose to be themselves
You would get to enjoy a little bit of what someone else has to offer

differences

Just because they graduated,
It doesn't mean you are failing.

Just because they travel more,
Just because they have a nice car,
Just because they have a bigger house,
Just because they are getting married,
Just because they have more friends,
Just because they get more social attention,
Just because they can quote more scripture,
Just because they don't include you,
It doesn't mean you are failing.

Chin up
We all have our seasons,
It doesn't mean you are failing.

why not me?

Sometimes it feels like everyone's dreams but mine come true
Always left behind

labels

They will try to put a name to you just because of something
that you did that one time

Define you by your mistakes
Mark you by your weakness

Let's not be identified by the tags they put on us
    You don't have to be trapped by the decisions you made
    before
So go ahead and rip that tag off

Break the mould
And take on a new shape
Those labels are not your identity

I'm trying to listen to what God says about me
Who He calls me to be
But I end up listening to what they say about me

    People will call you a lot of things; put their own labels
    on you
    But will you answer to them?
    They will remind you of your past and try to keep you
    back there
    They will put their fears on you, put their failures on you
    What will you choose to believe?

I tell you what, you don't have to believe or answer to them
Break that pattern

Don't settle for less
Don't allow what they say about you change the way you
see yourself
Because they will always have their opinions

And we can't let them decide what our opinions should be

focus

I blew over the spoon, eager to scoff down my food.

As I waited for my food to cool down, I noticed her sitting in the corner opposite the door.

I could see she had extra pieces of food that I must have missed. Where did she get it from?

Her plate looked more flavoursome than mine.

Dissatisfied with my choices, I quickly rushed to grab more food before they run out, leaving my plate on the table.

Within minutes, the girl had finished her food and was reapplying her lip-gloss and fixing her hair.

In those short minutes, my food became cold and had lost its kick.

Cold rice is not the one.

Time wasted focusing on others and what they have, when what we have chosen is enough for us.

First of all, finish what's on your plate before going for more.

Secondly, focus on your own plate.

Sometimes we forget to admire what's in front of us because we're too busy trying to get something better.

Do you ever get food envy? Cos I sure do.

Some else's food choices always seem better than mine.

Some else's life choices always seem better than mine.

Greed kills contentment.
Comparison kills contentment.

When you are focusing on someone else's journey, that means you've taken eyes off your own journey right?

I'm talking about when you're in your own world and life is going great. Then you glance down for a second and get caught up with what's going on around. You didn't intend to, but now you're not sure about your decisions anymore.

Don't worry about the direction they take.
It's okay to look up to someone.
They should influence you to do better.
Not stray you away from your own vision.

Stay loyal to your own vision.
Eyes up.
Focus.

Activity
Let's take a moment to focus on our goals

Goals to focus on for this week?

1.

2.

3.

Goals to focus on for the next six months?

1.

2.

3.

Goals to focus on for the next year?

1.

2.

3.

influential

Don't undermine the influence you have on people
People are always silently watching
They may not comment
Or give you credit
But they are paying attention to you
You inspire others and you don't even know it
Some may not want you to know it
You don't need a stage to be influential
So carry on as you were
People need you whether you know it or not

pace

I have to keep reminding myself that not everyone is growing and learning at the same pace as me.

I have to remember that those who are ahead of me should be a source of inspiration and support, not a source of jealousy and discontentment.

I have to remember to show love and patience to those who grow slower than me.

And, most importantly, I have to remember to make people feel safe and free to grow at their own pace.

stuck

It looks like everyone is moving forward but me

So I try to have a mentality like them
I try to grind like them
I try to be on it like them

I put all my effort in
So I too, can move forward and keep up with the world
But I end up empty
Chasing my own tail

I look around and I haven't moved an inch
I'm stuck in a timeline I should have left behind months ago
I see Him do everything I want for others
And it's driving me to the ground

I'm worn out
And I feel like I'm ready to settle

Will I die feeling empty?

I cried out to God, "Why are you letting everyone else move on but me?"
He told me, "I'm going to do things differently with you."

nothing to do with me

It's not personal
Everyone has a bad day
Sometimes a week or a month

Don't be offended when they
Don't smile back
Don't text back
Give you a cold shoulder

You try to remember what you did wrong
Your mind frantically reading into everything
Was it something I said?
Something I did?

This has nothing to do with you
Not everything is about you
It's about them
Take yourself out of it

Assumption is the worst free drug to dabble in
You're drowning in assumption, can't you see?

They are busy dealing with things
They may have stopped smiling because to them there's
    nothing to smile about
They may not text you back because they don't have the
    strength to do it

They may not know how to express themselves anymore

The person you once knew is still there
Not right now as they are dealing with other things

And now I feel selfish
Cos I was too busy judging you for not returning my phone calls
In my feelings because I felt ignored
Meanwhile you were hurting

Let's not play the tit for tat game
That game we all play
"If they don't text me, I won't text them."
"If they don't call me, I won't call them."
You're most likely playing alone

Be the first to reach out even though there is a possibility of being rejected
Swallow that pride of yours
Don't be the "I was thinking about calling you" type of person when it's too late
Swallow that pride of yours

be sensitive

Even the most confident people you know face battles that you'll never know about

It may look like they have it all together, but everything's crumbling inside

Don't be quick to assume that their lives are perfect and they don't need you

Don't dismiss their cry for help because you think they don't have any problems

They are just better at being okay in front of people

They still need your love and support
They still need your attention

Some people just prefer not having their problems out on display
And it's okay, we all deserve privacy

Be sensitive
Be compassionate
Be approachable

So they feel safe to come to us, and tell us that everything's not fine
It's heartbreaking watching the ones we love fall apart

It's even worse when they fall apart and can't confide in you

But we have to wait for them to open up
Don't force people to open up, that's not genuine
And you wouldn't want that for yourself either

Be as close as they want you to be

And, if this happens to be you, find comfort in a trustworthy friend
Because you don't have to go through things alone

it can be you

You've got to remember that in this life we are bound to encounter storms out of our control
"That can never be me," they say

Storms will knock on your door too
Sooner than you thought
And knock you off balance
Leaving you thinking "I never thought it would happen to me"

I tell you, you would be a fool to assume that a storm will never come your way
Because life has a way of humbling us
So humble yourselves
Before life humbles you

what they do

She smirks
  She glares
  She mocks you

  He bumps into you
  He mimics you
  He judges you

  They watch you
  They isolate you
  They belittle you

  Then they tell you they love you and it was all in your head

  Don't be too quick to dismiss your gut instincts, you're
  not being dramatic

    Their behaviour will always tell you how they feel
    about you
  Because actions always speak louder than words

Body language has move volume than the mouth

entitlement

I came to understand that just because you are entitled to
something, it doesn't mean that the world is obligated to
give it to you.

Have you ever helped a friend/loved one out in their most
difficult time and find that they didn't reciprocate when
you needed help?

You made a choice to help them.

And, just as you made a choice, they can make the choice to
not return the favour.

They don't have to.

I know it sounds hypocritical and you're probably thinking it's
disloyal. But just as no one owes you anything, you don't
owe them anything either.

Just because it's the norm, it doesn't mean it's an obligation.

A good friend would, of course, come to your aid when you
need it, some because they generally care about you. And
others because they feel obligated.

This makes me wonder whether the reason we feel entitled to
things is because we do things for others in the hopes that
they will do it back.

Realistically, people will put their needs before yours.

People will always put their needs before yours.

Not always maliciously, but because sometimes we need to put
ourselves first, so we can help others.

If we were both drowning, I need to save myself first then
come and help you, it only makes sense.

I have come to think of life to be like a zero-hour contract.

Nothing is guaranteed.

You're free to do what you want.

I'm saying don't get angry when you feel like someone was supposed to help you but didn't.

It's a hard pill to swallow.

celebrate your victories

Just because something's important to you
It doesn't mean it's as important to others

Don't be discouraged when they don't show the same
excitement as you do

Don't be discouraged when your expectation of their reaction
doesn't live up to what you imagined
And don't assume other people value it too

If it's important to you, make sure you celebrate it and not
dismiss it because others are not reacting in the same way

Celebrate alone if you have to

Don't dismiss your victories

big hearted

"Above all else, guard your heart, for everything you do flows from it." Proverbs 4:23

Let me tell you about having a big heart.
People will try to take advantage if you let them.
Have boundaries.

They'll start to expect things from you.
Even when they don't deserve it.
Have boundaries.

Not everyone carries a heart like yours.
Have boundaries.

Activity: Mindful Colouring

miss you

It's not you they miss
It's what you can do

They are attracted to the things you can offer more than they
are to you

balance

I know you're busy finding yourself

But we need to find a balance between the Me vs Them mentality

I don't understand why we try to fall at either end of the spectrum and not in the middle

Selflessness vs selfishness

Because there's no point of finding happiness if you don't want to share it with anyone

And what's the point of losing yourself for others?

So, feel free to go underground to find yourself, but when you come back, check in with your loved ones

And if they don't accept the new you, let them be

when they don't understand

Some people don't have bad intentions they just don't understand what you're doing.

And no matter how much you explain, it won't make sense to them.

They may never understand why you do what you do.

And they may seem like your opposition.

Don't be discouraged.
Don't compromise so it's easier for them to accept what you are doing.

Don't be upset that they don't appreciate all of your efforts and hard work.
At the right time, the right people will notice.

Be loving in your response.

As long as what you're doing makes sense to you.

Keep working at it.

Eventually, they'll understand.

The long run

There isn't a first-place prize on life
Everyone's running their own race

Your fitness journey
Your career
Your relationships
Your life

We don't all cross the finish line at the same time or place
So stop competing with others
And enjoy your run
You'll experience so much grace this way

And why are you running?
Are you doing it just to beat them?
Did you even stop to notice the treats life has offered to you?
Don't just passively run around until your time is up
It's like going on an Easter egg hunt and leaving all the eggs behind at every station
What's the point?

In your last days you should want to be able to look back and smile at the memories you made along the way
You don't want to get to the end exhausted and realise that you missed so many opportunities at being happy

relationships

break up

How do you know when it's time to walk away?
You've never done this before, and you don't know how to do it.
So, you turn to your friends for advice.
They tell you to do what feels right.
But that's not what you really wanted to hear.
Leaving you back to square one because you were secretly hoping they would tell you what to do.
Weeks of sadness turn into months.
Still no action taken.
A few minutes of being uncomfortable can save you months of heartache.
All it takes is for you to make that decision.
Just walk away.
But it's easier said than done.
Being unhappy is your new drive to do what you should have done a long time ago.
And now you're blaming them for how you're feeling.
Every time you look at them, they just remind you of how much of a coward you are.

He didn't do anything wrong.
And I wish I had a better reason.

Just walk away, Eve.
But love's sticky.

I held on because I thought things would get better.

They didn't.

Waited because I felt guilty for running away.

I spent so long drowning in sadness, and I couldn't lift myself out of it.

You don't see how bitter you've become. And justify this by saying you're unhappy.

Is that a reason to be cold?

You become the bad guy.

Blaming him for not knowing what's going on in your mind.

Yeah, I deserve happiness.

After weeks of finding the right words.

Now you're ready. But the timing's not right.

So, you wait some more because you're considerate.

Then the day arrives.

And you can't even stomach a spoonful of food.

Fumbling for the right words.

You already know how it's going to end.

He's going to be heartbroken.

And I can only blame myself for waiting so long to do this.

empty

I loved you the best I could
Until there was no more love
Let's both move on
My love for you run empty
And I have to ask myself, was it really love in the first place?
Because true love is endless, right?

the last days

You kiss me on my cheek.
"I love you."
I pretend to yawn to avoid responding.
"Today's been lovely." I say, avoiding eye contact.

Another yawn.
I have to pretend I'm sleepy, so you don't feel bad.
    I don't want to lie.
I can't do this anymore.
    I think our journey has come to an end.

time's up

I knew our time was up when you asked me "what we will
  name our kids?"
And, for the first time, I couldn't imagine starting a family
  with you.

let's not be friends

The day I let you go
You made me feel like I was the bad guy
And I took it
But I felt so free
A heavy weight lifted from my chest

You asked if we could still be friends
I said yes, I broke you, so it was the least I could do

But it was a big mistake
Because you still treated me like we were together

And now we can't be friends anymore
Because it wasn't a mutual decision
And you were still in love
Hoping we would get back together

It was a big mistake
I need to know that you aren't in love with me anymore

There's just too much history between us
And we can't jump back from that line that we crossed
I gave this friendship a chance
I gave you a chance
But you started to act a little cray cray
A little bit possessive
If we stay like this, I'll start to hate you

And we can't end things on hate
So let's not do anymore damage and just preserve what we had

And go our separate ways
Let's not be friends
It's better this way

venom

I know somewhere you've painted me as the heartless snake
who broke your heart.

I'm not okay with it.
But I understand.

all I do

I couldn't stop thinking about you yesterday
    And the day before
    And the day before that

I should find better things to do with my days
    But I don't want to

Falling for you gives me joy
    I just want to think about you
    And your beauty

    It's all I ever do

That's all I ever want to do

library

Who knew you could find love at the library
Instead of revising, I play that game when I stare at you for as
    long as I can without you noticing

You wear your white T
That makes me drool

I have exams to revise for
But I'm studying you

There are creases on your forehead as you tap away on your
calculator
Oough "He must be smart."

I try to be a cute stalker
And when you catch me looking
I smile, my crooked teeth front and centre

The next day I take a seat next to you
You have to notice me

I'm closer now
And you smell good my love

I spread all my books over the table
You have to notice my name written on top

I lean over and whisper, "Hey, I see you here every day, what are you studying?"

My heart racing
Blood boiling beneath my skin

We spoke for what felt like forever
Such a magical moment

You were kinder than I thought
And I knew you would be right for me

I look down the book aisle, and at the end my friend was watching me

I gave her that cheeky wink
Girl, you know what's up

hey handsome

I looked him in the eyes
Then handed him a note and told him he was handsome
Creepy
    My legs felt like jelly as I walked away
    I could feel his eyes on me
Then I just wanted to evaporate

drawn to you

I keep wanting to speak to you
I'm just too shy
There's something about you that turns me into a mute

If I stare at you longer, hopefully you'll get the message
But I can't even maintain three seconds of eye contact with
you

There's something about you, I can't put my finger on it
You're different from the others
You're so mysterious

I like your confidence
I like your style
I like how you kindly you speak to others, that's what drew
me in.

I wanna be yours

Would you love me if
I was more like her
More sporty?
More dressy?

What is your type?
Am I your type?
I know I am

On paper I tick all of your boxes
You're the only one that doesn't see it

Hahaha, no; I'm the only one that sees it

In my imagination
Completely sprung

I'm in that zone guys
This is a rocky place to be stuck in

But seriously, am I your type?
Cos I wanna be yours

Activity: Mindful Colouring

He loves me, He loves me not.

I took a shot

I took a shot
And you left me on 'read'
Ouch

A few hours later, I went to check
And you blocked me
Double ouch

Then I remembered that I easily do this to other guys without
a care
I shouldn't dwell on it

Moving on
It's actually empowering to make the first move
But for me it's more fun to be chased

one sided love

I haven't been on your social page for a while
I checked and the last time we spoke was two weeks ago

Who knew how powerful one-sided relationships were?

Had to mentally break it off
Before it mentally broke me off

I wouldn't call it love
Strong feelings

Feelings that had me believing we were meant to be
I'm still laughing at my stupidity

overestimation

I overestimated my importance in your life
Again
    I thought I meant something to you
    All you've taught me is that I'm too quick to follow my
    emotions

I'm a fool sometimes
And that's what happens when you *like* like someone
You let your imagination run wild

Let me pop the kettle on
A cuppa should ease my feelings
Come on, Eve

all of a sudden

I woke up one morning
And all of a sudden
You weren't my first thought

I shut my eyes and forced myself to daydream about you
But nothing happened

I couldn't think of you
My morning routine was disrupted

My inside screaming with joy
The Lord knows how many times I've tried to forget about you

Telling myself that one day I'll be over you
But secretly looking forward to our lunch dates in my dream

I'm glad you're not on my mind anymore

It was nice loving you
But this is goodbye

crushes

I liked you before I got to know you

Turns out that your crush is not the charming person you
    thought they were
That he is obsessed with his appearance
And she is beyond stingy
Some crushes are better off remaining as crushes
Because once you find out the truth about them it ruins all the
    magical daydreams you were planning on having

Because now you can't dream about the moment they'll kiss
    you
Or your wedding day
And not even the kids you'll have together

You don't have to pursue every crush you have
Sometimes admire people from afar
They'll never live up to what you hoped they'll be
So
They're better off being your fantasy

living life without you

I used to think I would never get over you
But look at me
Living life without you

How I tortured myself when you didn't reply
Or when I fretted about other girls talking to you

Sometimes I think about you
And I wonder if you're happy

But my heart is at peace
A calmness I never got when you were around

I heard you're married now
I hope she makes you happy

I hope you give her that sense of calmness I never got to
experience with you

family

You don't choose your family
But I was given a special one

We all have our own way of thinking and doing life
But we're still there for each other, even when we don't agree
with each other

And that is beyond special

the other half of me

It's a cold day in winter, and there is a family gathering happening. Everyone's catching up with each other as the house becomes hot and stuffy. It's so nice hearing stories from your older cousin's and seeing your uncle's new television that he just loves and talks about at every moment. The day is full of laughter, which extends late into the night. It is well past midnight, and your cousins go back to your house for a sleepover with you.

You love this as you crave a 'girls' night in. Cuddling on the sofa beds watching movies.

On the way home, you're half asleep and there's a smile on your face as you think about how much you love your family. It's always special when you spend time with them.

But there's a part of you that still feels incomplete. You shake this feeling off and try to enjoy the moment.

As you're getting ready to go to bed, your younger cousin – the one with no filter – asks, "Where's your dad?" I know, right, kids are random.

You think back to the time that you tried to ask that question but got ignored.

Maybe this is it. You think you might get the answers to something you wished to know.

There's a moment of silence as you secretly pretend to not be listening.

"It's late, go to sleep." is all she said.

For a few years I put this behind me. Why should I care?

It's because I have a circle that's half shaded, and I don't know what to do with the other side that's empty.

Why do I find myself thinking of someone who refused to know me?

Maybe it's because the other side of me is left unshaded and I want to fill it in with something.

Now I'm older I've come to learn that adults are complicated.

The situation was complicated.

Life's complicated.

I was the complication.

you left

Something's missing
I feel like I missed out on something special

I just want to ask him, what happened?

I had it all planned out
The day I would get to meet you
Finally reunited, after all these years
You would hold me up like the most beautiful person
you've ever seen

You would take me out and tell me why you left
And I would forgive you
Welcome you back with open arms that were never crossed

I had it all planned out
    "My little girl." he would cry
    He would hug me and tell me he's sorry
It would be a real love story
    And just like that
    I would forgive him

He was never a part of my life
    And now he never will be

A daughter's desire for a father
They say girls go after guys that are like their dads
Okay, so now where does that leave me
Wanting to know more about the man who left his responsibilities

Nah, I'm sure he regretted leaving
    Surely he thought of me
    Wondered what I looked like
    If I took after him

    Or if I was I the mistake he wanted to erase
    The shameful part of him that he prayed to forget

    For some reason, you left
    Did you feel like you weren't good enough?
    Or was I not good enough?

    I thought by now I would be over this

    It's weird
    Blinded with tears over a relationship that could have happened
    It's weird
    Mourning for a person that I didn't even know
    It's weird
    Grieving over a missed opportunity that will never come again

    You've left me twice now

They say you can't miss what you never had, but I miss the person I created in my mind

And now I'm stuck in a loop
The same questions going around in my mind
What if?

a letter to...

I don't want to take you for granted.
I love you.
I don't tell you enough.
But I do.
But I'm hurt.
You hurt me.
And I feel like you don't love me.
I don't agree with how you made your decisions.
And I did lose my faith in you.
You told me you loved me, but your actions told me that my feelings didn't matter.

Why is it so much easier to dwell on the love that we are not getting?
Than to recognise the love that we're not giving

Torn between respecting you and hating you.
I don't want to hate.

Did I hurt you?
I can see you are hurting too.
The amount of times I wanted to comfort you, hug you, tell you we will be okay in the end.
We will be okay in the end.

I feel sorry for you.
I feel sorry for me.
We both have to live with the decisions you made.

Are you happy?

you good?

They say to check up on your friends

But the only reason I don't always
Is because I feel like I'm bothering them

And I don't want to come across as clingy or needy

Is that selfish?
I guess so, cos I'm making it about me instead of about them

when the curtain falls

I'm disappointed in you.
You let me believe that we were friends.
But it was always about what you could get from me.

Yes, I'm in my feelings.
My heart is broken.

Yes, I'm angry.
I feel used.

Okay, I get it.
Not everyone you know is your friend.
But.
Dang.
You really ran a number on me.

I can't believe I trusted you.

I told you what kept me awake at night.
And you prayed for me.
You even wished blessings onto my life.

I thought I felt a spiritual connection.

Did you mean any of it?

Was it all just for show?

This whole time I've been getting cosy with wolves.
Playing with their fur.
Tickling their bellies.
Not knowing that they long to take a lunge at me.

Your mask accidentally fell off.
You placed it back on again, but it's crooked now.
I can see the real you hiding behind that mask.

But now I know the truth.
And it hurts.

I'll be fine eventually.
After I get over this shock.

I should have known better.

second choice

Being the other person
Being number two
The "Oh, you'll do for now" person
The "I don't have any more options" person

We can tell you know
I can tell I was your second choice

When the person you really want isn't available, so you settle
for another

Me

It hurts

I hate being your second choice
What am I doing wrong?

Wait

This isn't about a boy if you're wondering

It's about friends who holler only when they don't have
anything better to do
Or, when they remember you only when they need something
from you
The ones who come to you when no one else is available

Or, they have your name in mind; just in-case their first option cancels

Making you feel like the backup
The second choice friend

"I need to prove that I…"
"No babe, you don't need to prove anything."
"So what is it? What is it that I don't have?"
"Maybe you need new friends. Better friends."

It makes me feel used
Like there is a better alternative to me
But as for now, I'm better company than no company

I'm over it now

I don't have the desire to be anyone's second choice

So please don't disturb me with your insincere invites

The answer will be no

divine friendship

In search for a community.
A desire for real love.

To be known.
To be seen.
To be loved.

Something that I craved.
Friendships that will encourage my spiritual growth.

Tired of growing alone.
Tired of encountering the wrong people.

Have you ever felt out of place?
It's like you've just walked into a movie.
Everyone's playing their part.
And it feels like you're the only one without a script.
You feel lost.
You don't fit in.
And don't know who to turn to.

Everyone plays perfect.
They look good, they smell good and they're doing just fine.
And here you come along, dragging your baggage.
Wanting someone to help you carry the load.
But they seem busy.
And you don't want to impose.

It's funny how people become unconsciously exclusive.
Their mouths say, "You're welcome here." but their actions say something else.
Loving the idea of 'Come as you are', but as long as you come as how they want you to be.
Feeling the pressure to become perfect.
I thought I had to act right before tagging along.

Acting out of character in an environment that's all about truth.
The pressure to fit in is turning me less true to myself.
And I thought they could see right through my imperfections and know I'm not worthy.

I got tired of "almost" friendships that I stopped trying.
Started to do life alone.
Growing alone.
Then I got really comfortable doing it all alone.

But we're not meant to do life alone.

Sunday in.
Sunday out.
Going through the motions.

A stranger in a crowd.

I told God I would wait for his timing, but at that point I was just saying it to make myself feel better.

I made a mistake though.

Searching for people to fill up my holes instead of the One who will make me whole.

In my search for a Godly community, I made it all about myself.

All about what I needed.

Putting my expectations on people based on my needs.

Expectations even I fall short on.

I came to realise that no one's perfect.

Suddenly, one Sunday, a girl approached me, asked if I would like to sit with her.

And so I did.

I wasn't expecting much, maybe just company for that service.

I learnt not to expect much.

Sometimes it feels easier to have no expectations because people don't always mean what they say and, at some point, will let you down.

Then, the next Sunday she saved me a seat.

And the Sunday after that.

And the Sunday after.

I didn't see it coming.

I didn't even realise it when it happened.

But I'm not a stranger lost in a crowd anymore.

It took some time, but I'm with the right people now.

All I can do now is pay it forward.

And be the person that I needed for someone else.

Activity
Connecting

Creating meaningful friendships gets harder with age, as we find ourselves having to juggle work, family, 'me' time and social time. I've written a few suggestions that have helped me to stay in contact with people that I value. I know that some people are only in your life for a season, but, for those special ones, I do my part and make an effort in staying connected.

1. **Text/call a few people you haven't checked up on, or have lost touch with.**
   It could be friends/family who you are still close to but you find yourselves too busy to meet up/talk to each other.

   Or it could be a person you haven't spoken to in the last six months.

   It doesn't have to be anything super-deep, you could start by saying, "Hey, how have you been, thinking of you today." then let the conversation flow.

2. **Check in on your parents/carer/guardians/elders.**
   Things may look fine on the outside, but you might not know what's really going on with them unless you take the step and ask. And just because they are older than you, doesn't mean that they have passed the stage of going 'through things'. Everyone deserves to feel connected to someone, no matter the age.

3. **Meet up with someone and do something (eat out – try a new food joint, explore a city or town nearby).**

Find an activity that you both enjoy doing. Get some fresh air and experience something new. If you want to see someone but you're anxious about what to talk about etc, the cinema is a good place to start.

4. **Go on that date.**

   Dating doesn't automatically mean you're in a committed relationship. Don't be scared.

5. **Group outings**

   There are plenty of opportunities to connect with new people in a larger environment. There are many communities to join that can cater to your social, work or religious needs.

   Find people with similar interests; for example, if you like to ice skate but none of your immediate friends are keen on it, then you can join an ice-skating community where you will find people who would love to ice-skate with you.

6. **Start listening more to those around you; make them feel loved, heard and valued.**

we used to

So, I've learnt that I don't have to know the reason why you don't like me.

    I'm told that it shouldn't matter whether people like me or not.

    But you were my friend.

Even when we were friends, I saw how you sometimes looked at me.
    How sometimes you would belittle me.

But I blamed it all on my emotions and perception. Told myself I was being dramatic.

I always checked in on you.
    You stopped messaging me.
    Calling me.
    I thought that was just adulthood separating us.
But it was you distancing yourself from me.

You were my friend.

    There are some friendships that die out and there is peace in both your hearts. This one disturbs me because I was drastically cut off.

And I guess it bugs me cos you're still in deep contact with those around me.

Did I do or say anything to upset you?

We're down to birthday messages only. And it's awkward now.

Tell me.

It's personal now.

a letter to a friend

These last few weeks have been very difficult for me and having you by my side has been a blessing.

By sharing your own personal experiences with me, you have helped me make sense of some of my own thoughts, emotions and experiences which I subconsciously repressed. That was very kind of you.

I feel as if I am more objective in the way I deal with problems now; as in, you've reminded me to always look at the other side whenever I'm in a bad situation. I've learnt that just because someone is hurting me, it doesn't necessarily mean that they want to do it; they may be a victim of their own problems and I'm just collateral. It isn't fair for any of us. But c'est la vie.

I know that sometimes when we chat I can be quiet, but honestly, it's because I enjoy listening to you speak. I respect you; you take the time to help and your advice comes from a modest place.

For the first time this week, I opened up to my friends and told them everything about me and what I've been going through. I felt so bare, but I did not feel judged at all.

We're all afraid of being or even looking vulnerable and end up detaching ourselves from certain aspects of our lives that we don't like or even know how to express. Sometimes, you think you are so unique that the problems you are facing no one else will ever face, as they are personalised to you only. So, you think that talking to others may be a waste of time because, surely, they will never be in your shoes. The old line "talk to someone" might be clichéd, but when you speak to someone who cares and wants to help, you'll find yourself breaking through obstacles you branded as impossible. And you will feel awesome!

I will forever be grateful, and I hope I can be there for you in the same way.

You rock!

I love you

Eve x

Appreciation letter

Set some time to write a letter to someone to someone who has really been there for you.

Let them know what they mean to you and how their input has helped you.

Encourage them and let them know their hard work is appreciated.

old times

Do you remember when we were younger?
We would spend the whole day in school together
Then after we would spend hours on the phone to each other
We would watch TV together
Stayed up late revising for our exams together
Sometimes we wouldn't even speak but just knowing you were
on the other side of the phone was enough
I'm glad we did childhood together

And now we're older
And we don't spend as much time on our phones anymore
But when we do, it feels like we're picking up from old times

And when I'm hurt
Or struggling
Or having a hard time adulting
You're the first one I call
I'm so glad we're doing adulthood together

on your behalf

I failed to speak up for you
To stand up for you

Though I didn't say anything bad about you
And I didn't agree with what they said
My silence spoke for me

But sometimes I just let loud people talk
It felt pointless to add my voice because they would just
think that I'm trying to start an argument by standing up
for you
Not everyone knows how to 'agree to disagree'

But that's not an excuse
I should have said something

Next time I'll be loud for you
Because I've found my confidence now
I've found my voice

And you can rest knowing that I will defend you even when
you are not in the room

next time

    I'll be a better friend next time
I'll be there when you need some encouragement

I'll be there sitting on the front row, cheering you on

I'll also be there to give you some tough love

To let you know how you could do better

I did a lousy job last time

We're only human and bound to make mistakes
In this lifetime, you don't get to do things over again
Once it's done, it's done

But I can do things differently next time
And I want to be there for you

abandoned

I'm upset with You

Because You didn't do what I thought you would do

You got me excited to do something that you had no intentions
of being a part of

I wish I didn't put my all into it

You saw me rehearse

You know it's something that I wanted to do

The day was so disappointing, because my expectations didn't
match up to what I had planned

I feel like You abandoned me
I thought that God was sending me somewhere
But He didn't come through

And now I'm confused

Because I thought I was doing something He wanted me to do

I thought He gave me confirmation

And now I'm just left disappointed

And I'm trying to believe that He has better plans than what
I imagined

And I should be patient and just wait

I'm sat here wondering what happened
Maybe my motivation was not pure enough

But how long do I have to wait?

What do I have to do?

How come You didn't come?

Let's be honest; I'm angry

I kept asking You to be there

Because I know I couldn't do it without You

You knew I couldn't do it without You

How come You didn't come?

I'm so angry with You

What was the point?

Tell me

You probably have all the best intentions, but I just feel like you've left me down

I don't even want to talk to You right now

Goodnight

to the One above

Each day I trust You a little bit more
Each day my love for You grows
I now understand what it means to be in a relationship with
     You

I'm sorry for the times I doubted You
I was so consumed in my version of my future
But Your plans have always been better than mine
And You know exactly what I need
You've always had my best interest
Even when I had been selfish

And I'm so glad that You were the one that captured my heart
Because I know You will never abuse it
I'm putting all of my trust in something bigger than myself

I only ask You to teach me how to love the way You love
Help me show grace towards others just as You've shown grace
     towards me

the sheep that strays

When you haven't prayed for a while
And it feels awkward
Because you feel guilty
For forgetting about Him
Turning your back on Him

Cos now it feels like you're only going to Him because you
need something
And well, it is kind of true

And it feels foreign
Saying you love Him
You do mean it
But you haven't been showing it
You've been distant for a while
Disconnected from Him

I have to admit I was gallivanting around the streets
But I'm going back home to Him now

"I'm sorry; please don't give up on me. I've been reckless."
That's all I can say for now

learning curve

I'm busy

We don't need to be doing everything to feel important.

Keeping busy to mask our loneliness.
Keeping busy to look like we have it all together.
Feeling like you always need to do more.

Why am I always so busy?

To be honest, there was a point in my life when I kept myself
    busy because I didn't know what I really wanted.
A cluttered mind.

I thought I was keeping myself open to new opportunities.

Juggling three jobs and involving myself in different activities
    on the side.
At first it was going so well, I felt accomplished each week.
Proud.
But distracted.

Looking back, I now understand that I was actually running.
Distracting myself from pain and feeling like a failure.

Being busy for the wrong reasons.
Intentionally staying busy so I'm not left alone with myself.

There were a lot of tears of hopelessness.
Endless prayers for wisdom and clarity.

I had to learn to be compassionate towards myself.

Slowly focusing on what's important to me.
Less noise.
Being busy for the right reasons.
There are days when I feel unproductive, and that's when those
    unavoidable feelings come to play.

Just like me, you too have to learn to ride out those moments,
    and resist the urge to run away from them.

say no

I used to be such a yes girl.
Saying yes too quickly.
Pressured into it.
Not wanting to offend.
And sometimes being guilt trapped into accepting.

I didn't have the heart to say no.
But, at the end of the day, I was the only one suffering because
    I was doing something that I didn't necessarily want to do.

Limiting myself more than helping others.

Left feeling conflicted because, yes, I do want to help, but at
    the same time I don't always want to get involved.

Left feeling guilty.
Saying yes with resentment.

You know it's time to make a change when it eats at your heart.
The first few times I put my foot down and said no, I was
    called a few names, but to be honest the freedom I got
    from it is something I'm willing to pay for.

If choosing to say no makes me happy, then that's a choice I
    will continue to take.

Some people will try to manipulate you.

But once I understood the cost of my freedom, saying no
    became easier.

Don't look at me differently.
I'm still a good person, I say yes when I can, and if I know that
    I am truly able to get involved.
But I refuse to say yes then bend over backwards trying not to
    disappoint anyone while being miserable doing it.

Be real with yourself, know that it's okay to say no.
Don't let anyone make you feel like you are being selfish.

You'll disappoint some people along the way.
But you've got to stand firm in your decisions.
Because people will make you feel bad, especially if it's an
    inconvenience for them.

Learn to say no without guilt.
Without a reason.

It's so freeing.

get some gas

You've got to have enough petrol in your car to keep it moving.
Because a car running on empty will not go anywhere, no matter how hard you press down on the acceleration pad.
A wise person always makes sure they have enough petrol in their car; how else will they drive to their destination?

If you keep trying to do everything without stopping to fuel yourself, eventually you'll stop moving.
But life will carry on, whether you're moving or not.

Don't let yourself run dry.

Let's do a check in.
Are you feeding yourself?
Physically, mentally and spiritually?

Are you surrounding yourself with people who will remind you to feed yourself?
Because sometimes we get so busy, we forget.

Take care of yourself first before anything else.

time out

There are some things that I don't need to see

So I'm just going to remove myself

From things that won't help me grow

From things that are distracting me

From things that will make me doubt myself and bring back
fear

From things that make me feel bad about myself

From people who are just negative

I'm taking some time out for myself

let loose

Without a care in the world
I closed my eyes
And let the beat guide me

The heat from the lights bouncing off my skin
Then it was just me and the song
Alone
My hands up in the air as I roll my body to the beat
Without a care in the world

Hundreds of people disappeared, and I was left free
I smiled to the rhythm
Swinging my arms right
Then left

The drumbeat guiding my waist
He makes me forget everything that's going on in my life
My lover for the night

In that moment, I found bliss in the weirdest place

pause before reacting

Advice to my younger self
Pause before reacting.
Waiting one more second can make a difference.
Not everything has to be immediate.

Did someone say something that upset you? Take a breather
then reply later.
You need to wait for your head to become clear.

Recognise the signs when you are about to react; is it your head
suddenly becoming hotter? Is it a sudden urge to click 'buy'?
    What is it for you?

For me, my thoughts float around my head fifty times quicker
than usual and I can't hear any other voices but my own and,
in the heat of the moment, I react.

But sometimes I feel numb, and feel pressured to feel
something, so I instantly react without thinking.

Don't be led by temporary emotions.

work in silence

I know you want to show them that you can do it
    That you've done what they said you couldn't
    You're proud of the work you've done
    I know you're excited

    But can you take that extra minute to just hold on and analyse your situation?

    Do you absolutely need to reveal it right now?
    Rushing has a way of ruining things

All it takes to ruin things, is to:
    Share it too soon
    Tell the wrong person
    Or present it in the wrong way

    Protect your craft in all stages
    The easiest way to knock you off course is things going sideways on a project you have invested in

    Work in private
    Cultivate in private
    Make sure your roots are deep and strong

    And when you're ready
    Share with the world

promises

Don't say things you don't mean
You'll make us doubt you
Even if you have the purest intention

a child that roars

A child that roars is a person who refuses to stay quiet, and uses their story as a source of strength for others. They stand firm even when they are in a position that exposes them to being shamed and judged. I applaud those who make that decision everyday.

When you strip off the mask and let yourself be vulnerable,
You're being brave.

After walking through the fire, you have a choice to make.

Let your vulnerability weaken and consume you.
Or
Use your vulnerability to strengthen yourself and others.

Hint: be brave enough to choose the latter.

life changing moments

David volunteered to battle the giant Goliath.

And I need that kind of confidence to challenge the Goliaths in my life.

But David learned to overcome the smaller battles first to protect what was his.

And since he won the battles before; he knew he could do it again.

So when Goliath stood tall.

David trusted in God's strength and in his own skills to defeat the giant.

It's the little wins that lead to greater wins.

Persevere in your small battles.

It's all preparation.

Our future is waiting behind our own Goliaths.

And we need to have the courage to challenge the giants in our lives.

a lion's attitude

A lion isn't the strongest or the biggest animal
But is the most feared

In their minds, they believe they are the most powerful
They fear no other animals
It's what makes them the rulers of the jungle

They are naturally brave
So you need to have a lion's attitude
It's your attitude that matters

You need to believe that you are capable and not reduce
yourself for less
It's your perception of who you think you are that matters

It's your mind that matters
Nothing is as powerful as your mind

forgiveness

One moment you feel like you have forgiven them
Then they breathe
And the pain and anger comes back
The memories of when they hurt you rush through your mind
Then you just wonder; will I ever look at them and not feel
like crying?

You have suffered enough
You keep waiting to feel like you have forgiven them

You want to set them free
You want to set yourself free
You don't want to live with the hurt anymore

How frustrating is it when you're mad at someone, and they
are just enjoying their life?
You just want them to acknowledge your pain
And for them to feel remorseful
And to be hurting just as you hurt
So that you can feel better
As if you got some justice

But the world doesn't work that way
And people will hurt you
And they won't care

Forgiveness is intentional
You have to try
It allows you to have power over your own life
Because when you don't forgive, they will have power over you

forgiving yourself

One thing about growing up is that you realise some of your old ways were not the best ways.

At the time, you thought you were doing what was best.

But now you've grown and realised that there were better ways of doing things, but you didn't know it at the time.

You couldn't have known.

So, you shouldn't hold yourself accountable for the things you didn't know.

So you have to forgive yourself for not knowing what you should have known.

You're still developing.

You can't change your past; you can only move on and do better.

And now you know better.

So, move on and do better with what you now know.

self love

You see when you fall in love with yourself,
Can you tell me what that actually feels like?

the art of taking responsibility

Taking responsibility is more than a pretty phrase we say

It's owning up to your mistake
It's coming face to face with your difficulties
It's knowing that you're not right all the time
It's knowing that you can do better
And not making up excuses for yourself

Taking responsibility for the choices you make is an ugly thing
It can be frustrating and uncomfortable

You must face the fact that you are responsible for the decisions
    that you make
It's not fair to us when you blame us for everything that goes
    wrong in your life
And although life may throw balls at us
It's how you react when you get hit that matters

If you ever want inner peace
You have to break the pattern of pointing the finger at everyone
    but yourself

No matter what your circumstances are
Yes they hurt you
Yes it wasn't fair
But what you do next is your choice

as your voice quakes

Speak the truth
Even when you're scared

Speak the truth
Even if it means disappointing someone

Speak the truth
Even if there's a chance you'll get in trouble

Small white lies matter
Because they can turn you into a bigger liar

Speak the truth
Because that's the right thing for you to do

interpretation

There is a difference between what someone said and what
    you hear.
I think our experiences and perception shadow our
    interpretation.
That's why I can say the same thing to two people and they get
    different meanings out of it.
So, sometimes it's better to clarify after having a difficult
    conversation with someone.

guidance

Lord, I pray for wisdom and clarity as you show me what's
   next.
I pray for peace during the times I find myself in situations out
   of my control.
I can't do this without your guidance
Don't let me get complacent
Revive and refine my dreams each time I lose focus

Who do you look to for guidance?

Activity: Mindful Colouring
Follow your heart

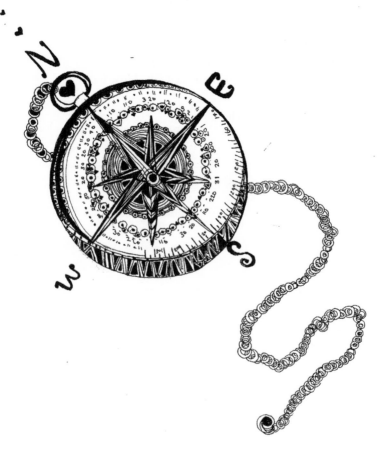

exposure

A little bit of exposure
Goes a long way

A few minutes a day out of your comfort zone
It's not a lot
But it could make a difference

A few minutes of doing what you fear
Could be the stepping stone you need

Baby steps

Get yourself used to being around your sharks
Things that you think would swallow you up

A little bit of exposure
 Are you gonna do it with me?
 Do new things
 Living on the edge

Knowing that you're scared right now but it will work out well
for your future

 Cos you know where you want to be
 And you know that means changing things from how they
 are now
 So, there's no point in delaying

transformation

You need to identify ways that will make a change to your life if change is what you desire.

For me, here are my transformation techniques that I focus on when I'm trying to make a change in my life.

Self-Discipline: Practising self-control and staying away from temptations.
Consistency: Showing up day in, day out. Even when you don't feel like it. You'll still put in the effort.
Resilience: Keep fighting. Bouncing back after things go wrong/not according to your plans.
Proactivity: Being intentional and taking action.
Inspiration: Surrounding yourself with the things that inspire you, to remind you of why you started.
Gentleness: Because sometimes we get it wrong and we mess up, so we must be kind to ourselves.

All challenging but doable.

spontaneous

You must challenge yourself
To stop planning everything
Trying to control everything

As the sun rises, let it be
Stop worrying about what other people will say
Step out and break your image of perfect
And play around your self-imposed boundaries

You want to shake the boredom out of your life
Then you'll need to practice living more spontaneously

You don't have to make it too eccentric
Yes, it takes courage to take big risks
But making small yet important decisions can make you
happier
Even small risks can be the most pivotal for your life

Start rolling your dice
And become comfortable with taking risks
Try something different

Activity
'Rolling the dice' game

Rules

Step 1: Write a bunch of new things you want to do on paper. Tear them out individually and put them in a hat/bowl.

Step 2: Randomly choose one and do what is written.

Step 3: Once you have done it, write down another new thing you'd like to do on paper and put it into the same hat/bowl.

Repeat the steps in order.

Enjoy new adventures.

You can make this a daily, weekly or monthly thing. That should get the ball rolling on being spontaneous... Then, maybe one day you won't need to play this game. You'll have the freedom to just wake up and do new things.

Below is an example of five different things someone could put down.

1 = try a new restaurant
2 = go ice skating
3 = dye your hair
4 = get a piercing
5 = visit the countryside this weekend

unwrapping

Unwrapping your gifts is a process

Sometimes our gifts are hidden or lost
    And we have to find them before we can unwrap them

    We might find ourselves frustrated as we tear off a layer
and we haven't discovered what's inside yet

    Then the layers of wrapping paper teach us to be patient
as we get closer to our gifts

    It's a shame to see people stop trying after a few layers
    Yes, it can be frustrating unwrapping and not seeing any
progress

    We shouldn't give up and stop unwrapping
    You'll be surprised by what you find
    You'll be surprised by who you find

approval

I'm not going to need anyone's approval anymore
    That's what destroyed me

I'm starting to believe in myself
And believing in God
I'm washing off the unhealthy need to be noticed
And living for an audience of one

You'll never know complete freedom if you still need to
impress others

I no longer need your okay so I can be okay
No longer waiting for others to stroke my ego
Slowly reeling myself off my necessity for others

I'm not expecting a round of applause anymore
    No longer revelling in their praises

That's the old me

If you want to clap for me go ahead, but just know I can go
without it too

taming the wind

I was a firm believer in 'going with the wind'.
Only planning certain things in my life.
My version of being efficient is looking at transport routes as
    I'm heading out the door.

Having had past plans go astray.
I stopped believing in planning.
And it was fun for a while.
Spreading the gospel of how freeing life is without any limits.
This is true to an extent.

Then things started to become repetitive.
I found myself going in circles.
Sleepwalking through life.

When I stopped to reflect, I realised that I didn't achieve many
    goals.
Realising I didn't have any goals in the first place.
I found myself being in the same situation I should have left
    years ago.

This made me think about what I actually want in life.

If you don't strive for anything you will get nothing.
Planning creates targets.
Targets that you can hit and achieve.

If you don't plan, you are shooting your arrows out to nothing,
therefore you won't hit anything.

For me, I'm learning to tame the wind.
I don't want to lose the part of me that's spontaneous.
And I don't want to live recklessly without some sort of
direction.

I won't let the wind direct my life anymore.
I won't walk around aimlessly.
This is me being an adult.
And taking ownership of my life.

So let's set some goals.

Goals for today.
Goals for tomorrow.
Goals for next year.

your energy is contagious

　　Look at your circle
What are their energy levels?
Are they always bitter and complaining
Or are they generous and loving

When you bring good vibes to the table
Watch as people bring their own chairs to sit with you
　　We love being around you
That energy you have, we all want some
Share please

environmental check

It's time to do a clean up
It's time to inspect
Get rid of all the things that are expired
Things that are reeking and leaving a stench in the air
That bad attitude
The inconsistency
The nasty habits
And so on

It's time to clean up your environment
The rotten people who you've placed on the front row of your
    life
The rotten thoughts you've allowed to camp in your mind
If you leave them there, they are bound to infect you

You want to be pure
You want to move on
You want your visions to come to fruition
But your environment is dirty
Your environment doesn't want you to grow
Your environment hoards fear, shame and sorrow
It's like whisking a fresh egg and a bad egg together and
    expecting it to be fresh; it will always end up rotten

Your environment should nourish you
It's time to restock
Replace the tainted with the clean

community

"A person standing alone can be attacked and defeated, but two can stand back-to-back and conquer. Three even better, for a triple-braided cord is not easily broken." Ecclesiastes 4:12 NLT

You'll go far if you surround yourself with like-minded people

You need people to stand for you when you can't bring yourself to stand
You need people who will believe in you when you can't believe in yourself
You need people that you can be honest with
You need people who will keep you accountable for pursuing your dreams

You shouldn't fight alone
We all need a support system
People to do life with

In a boxing ring, each player has a fighter's corner, and in that corner you'll find people who clean their bruises, give them water and show them where to attack their opponents so they can win the fight

Sometimes, when we're in a battle, our view becomes cloudy and we don't always make the best decisions but our support system is there to point us in the right direction

The enemy attacks the hardest when you are alone
The enemy wants to knock you out
That's why you shouldn't fight alone

Don't isolate yourself
Not being in a community is torture to our souls
We were designed to do life together
Surround yourself with the right voices

We're more powerful when we're together

mirror

If you stare at a mirror long enough, you begin to see more than a reflection of yourself.

What do you see?

Do you see the beauty in your eyes, your body, and your soul?

Or does your insecurities stare back and haul insults at you?

Go to the mirror and look at yourself
See who you are
Notice your strengths
See who you can be

See what other people see when they look at you
You're the greatest

Activity
Affirmations

Drop what you are doing and go to the mirror.
Look at it.
Then say ten kind things to yourself.
(If you're not close to one then use the black screen on your phone. If not available close your eyes and do it.)
Repeat every time you're in need of encouragement.

thank you

For never forgetting about me when all I do is forget you.

For making me your number one even after I dedicate the last few seconds of my day to you.

For loving me when I hated myself the most.

For blessing me even though I don't deserve it.

For providing me with food even when I didn't acknowledge that others would sleep without.

For forgiving my selfish and reckless ways.

For being patient with me even after I have failed you time and time again.

For sending your son to die for my sins, despite all I've done.

For giving me another chance.

For loving me.

For being love.

acceptance

Sometimes I waste my energy on things I know I can't change.
Other times I look back, even though I know moving forwards
is my best option.
It feels safer.
But why do we do this?
Hurt ourselves.
Unintentionally creating long lasting pain.
Struggling to accept the obvious.
I can admit that sometimes I don't want to accept the truth,
even though I am aware of it.
The truth isn't always what I want. Even when I need it.
I would rather feel sorry for myself for a while and then accept
the truth later.
When I'm ready.
Meanwhile, secretly hoping that things may turn around.
Being hopeful.
You will come across situations which you have no control
over.
It will make you feel powerless and, yes, it's frustrating because
there is nothing you can do.
So, when this time comes, be patient with yourself.
Decide that you are going to accept the situation as it is.
Whatever closure you think is owed to you, you may never get
it.
Why? I don't know, Hun.
Acceptance is a process.
It may take days, maybe longer.

Try not to force yourself, you will spend a lot of energy on it.

All this does is make your problems seem bigger than what they actually are.

And this energy will only make you focus on what you can't change.

Believe me. It can be exhausting.

Resisting acceptance can create anxiety.

Practicing how to accept will lessen anxious feeling and improve your self-awareness.

And self-awareness breeds the ability of seeing the situation from a different perspective. Which will help you in the process of moving on.

Some days you'll feel strong, content, lucky.

On others you'll feel angry, ashamed, hopeless.

It's going to be a rocky journey at first.

Especially since we live in an 'instant' era. It's something that simply can't be forced. You have to believe it.

And you have to work on it.

Acceptance doesn't mean giving up.

It opens you up to the truth. Reality.

Take time and be kind to yourself during this process.

fake supporters

It's the same people who doubted you who will turn around and ask you for favours

It's the same people who ignored you who will say you think you're better than them because you made it, when they were the ones who rejected you

It's the same people who didn't notice your worth and discouraged you who will want a share of your victory

Now that you're winning, they want to win too
But they didn't want to be a part of the process and get their hands dirty with you

Because some people can be selfish
And they only think of how you can help them
And if they don't see your value, they'll dismiss you
Because you can't give them what they want

But you've got to see your own worth
And not judge yourself by how they treat you

I'm trying to have a soft heart
And not hold on to bitterness

I'll be the bigger person
I won't do them as they done me
Our behaviour just exposes what goes on in our hearts
But I'm not going to be a doormat

can you handle it?

You've got to handle the pressure to cultivate your dreams

When you're under pressure you become vulnerable

You're sensitive to information around you

All your senses are heightened

And it's easier to be influenced

So you've got to be careful with who and what you surround yourself with at that time

Surround yourself with positive influences and people who want you to reach your goals

when you don't understand

Am I doing the right thing?
Because it doesn't make sense
I can't connect the dots

How are You going to get me there?
I know I shouldn't worry about the 'How's'
Because You got this

But I can't help but wonder
How will You do it?

I don't understand what I'm doing most of the time

But I still believe that in the end it will be great
I know what I'm doing is important to me

I'm going off from a desire that keeps pulling at me
I have to keep trusting myself
Keep trusting God
Especially on nights when I feel like throwing in the towel
And I have no one to tell me it will work
Because I can't even explain to others what I'm doing

I feel ridiculous sometimes, for following an idea that I don't
fully understand

But I didn't throw in the towel
I opened myself to learning more
One day at a time

The more I kept working on it
The more aware I became
The more my dreams became refined

And then the lights came on
Everything started to become clearer

failed

Even if it doesn't work out
You'll still be alright

It just depends on how you look at it
Most people look at it as wasted time

But I look at it as character building
This way it's not failing, it's progressing

It's the only way that helps me to move forward

leaving the door open

Once you've experienced rejection
It's easier to keep the door locked than to risk being rejected
again
It's happened before and there's a chance it might happen
again

It takes real strength to keep the door to my life open
When the fear of rejection is pulling in to close it

Who would want to be the fool that risks it again?

Me

Why?

What's the point of me trying?

Because if I keep that door locked, I'm scared I'll lose the key
And be locked away forever

Letting people in is a gamble
And I'll probably feel like a fool

But I'll take the risk
I'll leave the door slightly open
To let a little bit of light in my life

character building

It makes sense now
Life is trying to develop me as a whole
Making me face challenges every moment
Because He knows that I've got some areas in me I need to tighten up

All these locked doors in front of me
I know it's really a test of my heart
A test of my character

Whenever I feel out of my depth
Or I have no idea why hard things are happening to me
I change my perspective
I tell myself
"Easy child, it's only character building."
"You're going to be proud of yourself in the future."

But I'm tired of being in the examination room
Answering the same questions over and over again

I'm anticipating the kind of person I will be in the end

comfort zone

Are you willing?
To be vulnerable and start all over again

Are you willing?
To face everyone and admit that it didn't work out but you're
not giving up
Even when you hear the echo of their laugher

Are you willing?
To be brave enough to pursue your desire

Are you ready to leave your comfort zone?

Are you prepared for when things don't go your way?

Because it sounds all inspirational and stuff but it's really an
ugly internal war zone that births a beautiful person

when you feel like giving up

Your best won't come as easy as you might think.
To stop and quit now would be to spit all over everything
you've worked so hard to build.
You've come a long way.
I know giving up feels like the best thing to do right now.
Because sometimes it's easier to be a dreamer.
You have to fight that voice that tells you it's not worth it.
I know, I've been there.

You can't give up.

Cry.
Get angry.
Scream.

Let it all out.

Then get back on track.
Remember why you started.

premature

I don't want to rush things anymore
I've now learnt the value of waiting until it's the right time

I don't always get it right, though
But I wait and trust God in His timing
Because His day is delivery day

And sometimes it feels uncomfortable
Carrying something precious and wanting to reveal it to the
world

To hold it in your arms and show people the greatness you've
been carrying

But, just like pregnancy
I'm trying my best to not deliver prematurely

I don't want to risk the chances of its survival
Even though my mind and body tempts me to push

It's not my time yet
I'm not ready yet

So I sit
And wait
And nourish
And write

And grow

And feed myself with the right foods

Waiting for my due date

soaring

real me

I want to spend time with you
The real you

Without any add-ons
Or filters

You've spent years hiding them from everyone
But you can never hide you from yourself

The real you
The stuff you're not proud of

You think you don't deserve more
That you're a fraud
And if they knew who you thought you were, they would think
    less of you

But deep down. It's you who thinks less of yourself

When someone gives you a compliment, you can't even accept
    it, because you know they mean the person you play and
    not the real you

Even you don't know who the real you is anymore

And you wonder, will anyone ever think the real me is worth
    something
Because you still have some things to work on

The quest to knowing, understand and making yourself better
    is not as romantic as people make it out to be

Getting rid of your ugly habits is a painful life lesson

It's fighting yourself
Having to correct and retrain your mind against things that
    are not right, but are deeply woven into you

It's having to take a really good look at yourself and accepting
    all that you find
The good and the bad
It's having to take the risk to be your most authentic self even
    though there is a chance of being rejected

While you're running around trying to be someone else
Someone's waiting on you
They need you

So, let me get the chance to actually meet you
I mean the real you

And don't apologise for who we find

I know you've been working hard to get here

And you feel like you still have a long way to go

But please
Will you let me?

growth pains

If you want to grow
Expect to feel an uncomfortable stretch
For to grow is to expand
And expanding will dislocate old ideas; in order for new ones
    to take shape

As my mind stretches
One moment I'm feeling fulfilled
Then suddenly I'm feeling conflicted
All at the same time

The mood swings of growth
Questioning my abilities to fulfil my dreams

Your dreams need space to grow
You need to give yourself space to grow
So you have to keep yourself open to new ideas
Widen your capacity
And separate yourself from your victim mentality

I can see God's fingerprints all over this
This is what I wanted
What I prayed for
But birthing this dream feels like such a burden now
Restless nights as it grows bigger

I'm worried that I won't be able to handle it properly

What if I'm not the right person for this?

This dream is taking me to new and unfamiliar places
And it's uncomfortable
The side effects of following your vision

I have to have faith as I walk through this jungle of self-
    discovery
And be kind and gentle to myself as I work on my dreams
Especially when I feel lost or trapped

butterflies

Whenever I'm about to do something out of my comfort zone
My heart sinks down to my stomach
I can feel the butterflies fluttering wildly
My hands become slippery
And the toilet becomes my best friend

Because I know I'm about to step into a great opportunity

And it's scary
The unknown
Knowing that what I'm about to do brings discomfort but is necessary
Unaware of what the future holds
Will I make it?

I desperately want to see the best version of myself
Allowing myself to step into my fears is terrifying, for this moment
But I know that the future Eve will not regret it

Once you start doing it
Your focus shifts to giving it your best shot
The butterflies will still be there

You'll feel them multiplying
But it's a sign that you've broken out of your cocoon
And you're ready to fly

Activity: Mindful Colouring

What makes you feel like butterflies
are fluttering in your stomach?

I'm getting there

Things are starting to align.
I'm getting this fuzzy feeling in my heart.

I'm at the part where my past and my future are starting to
come together.
It hasn't happened yet.
But I can feel it.
I'm beginning to feel hopeful.
No, there's a better word…
Purposeful.
My story is to help others.
There was a time when I would spend the day crying in bed.
Asking God to show me where I'm going.
Not knowing that my purpose in life has always been there.
I just couldn't see it.
My vision distorted from comparing myself to others.

Feeling under qualified.
Not the right person.
What did I expect when my vocabulary was full of "I can't do
it, I can't do it"?
My "cannot" became my "would not".
I wouldn't because I thought I couldn't.

But I knew I was made for greatness.
I knew my current state was never going to be permanent.
This nagging feeling telling me to not give up.

Trusting that it would work out but having no idea how.
From a place of emptiness, I would thank God for what he is
about to do in my life.

I've always had the gifts.
I just wish I knew sooner.

when I get through it

After walking through fire...

I'll be a better daughter
I'll be a better friend
I'll be a better mentor
I'll be a better person

And I'll be stronger

I'll be a better me

first choice

Do you ever feel bad for doing what's best for you?
It's one of the hardest things to do
Because you have to let down a few people
Even those who you love

Sometimes being true to yourself is inconvenient to some people
Don't feel like you have to compromise yourself for others

Those who used to benefit from you making yourself second choice will say you've changed
You don't serve their selfish needs anymore

Don't feel bad about it
You owe it to yourself to take care of someone important
You

proactive

I would rather break a leg chasing an adventure
Than stay still and lead an unfulfilling life

make up your mind

Stuck on a mental treadmill
I got sick and tired of running and not going anywhere

Shrinking and lowering myself
Because I'm afraid of what will come out of me, if I decide
to step up

Fearful that my dreams would never live up to what I
thought they would be
That my dreams were a waste of creativity

Afraid of what will happen after I succeed
Will I ever do anything great after that?
Will I be a one hit wonder?

I got tired of settling for less
Reducing myself for less
I've made up my mind

Life changing decisions require you to be recklessly brave

I'm tired of talking about being bold someday
    I've made up my mind
    I'm ready to be about it

It's all or nothing
No matter the cost

picture it

I'm sat in Waterstones.
Looking directly at the bookshelf where my book belongs.

I can picture it sitting there.
And if I believe that it will happen.
Then it will.

Do you believe in vision boards? Maybe vision statements?

The first time I heard about it, I thought it was a magical time-wasting project. That just made you feel good about yourself.

I attended a masterclass in 2016 and created my first vision board.

The speaker was inspirational and shared her personal experiences, but even as I was creating my own board, I didn't exactly believe in it. I was just using it as a creative session.

The first thing that came to life was my safari trip. On my board, I simply had a picture of lions and cheetahs and I had 2017 written next to it. This came true the next year when I ended up going on an overland trip around Africa for almost three months.

At first, I didn't really believe they would happen. They were just pictures and words cut out from a magazine.

But constantly seeing the board just drew me closer. And I was reminded of the things I wanted most in my life.

You get what you focus on.

Every time I looked at my board, I could see my life goals staring back at me, encouraging me to take action.

I'm here to tell you that you need to visualise your future. Be clear in what you want.
Pay extra attention to the things that pull at you the most. Have a plan and watch as what matters to you most blooms in front of you.
Then place it somewhere you can see it, on your wall, diary, laptop or mobile screensaver.

I am a church girl and I believe that God made it possible for all of it to happen.

Whatever your beliefs are, I challenge you to picture all of your desires and then throw them all into a vision board/statement if you haven't done so already.

Add all that you want. Even if you think it's impossible.

It will be worth it.

there's time

There's still time to graduate

There's still time to travel

There's still time to go back and study

There's still time to switch careers

There's still time to buy a house

There's still time to lose weight

There's still time to gain weight

There's still time to fall in love

There's still time to say sorry

Things may never work out the way you plan for them to happen

I know you're scared of time running out on you

I wish I had a time machine too

To go back and make different choices

To make better choice

I know you're worried about all those missed opportunities

And the time wasted too

But they are old memories

You don't have to replay your past failures

If you're heart's still beating, then there's still time to make new memories

Choose to start now

short-changed

Short-changed: when you don't receive what is owed to you

The love you give them is not the same returned
The support you give them is not the same returned
Left feeling cheated
But life's not fair
You don't always get back what you give

People may short-change you, but don't make the mistake of
　　doing it to yourself
Don't sleep on yourself
You have to to give yourself everything that you try to give to
　　others
Love yourself
Invest in yourself
Believe in your own abilities

motivation

It's okay not to feel motivated

Don't think that to be successful you always have to be drugged
up in a motivated state
Because motivation alone won't finish your work for you
If you waited to feel motivated before you did anything,
chances are you would waste most of that precious time
waiting

You have to put in work even when you don't feel motivated
Do what you need to do even if you don't feel like doing it

There were days when I knew I only had a few chances to write
but at that time I didn't feel motivated
I still did what I had to do; my creative juices met me there

What you need to know, is that motivation requires action

dreaming big

Life can be scary.
Growing up can be scary.
There are so many things unknown to us.
But, in everything I do I try to be brave.

I've got more than one dream. And whenever I decide to go after one the thought of it makes my stomach hurt. All at the same time it excites me.

A dream that is intimidating yet electrifying.
Both feelings battling for my attention.

Do you have big dreams?
It doesn't necessarily have to be something dramatic.
But something that captures your heart.

What's stopping you from following them?

Some of the things that stopped me were:

1) I was afraid that my dreams weren't important enough and that they wouldn't help anyone.
2) I was afraid because I know there's someone out there who is 100 per cent better than me.
3) I was afraid to put all my efforts into something and it not working out, wasting my time.

I started to write so many years ago, but I stopped because I lost confidence in myself and eventually the flame died down. Hours that I will never get back. I stopped because I thought a person like me would never be an author. Like, who did I think I was?

But I didn't completely lose the flame, it was buried deep down. And it took a lot of digging, learning and self-reflection to bring that flame back.

I'm not going to quit my job and all of that to follow my dreams. If you want to (or if that's part of your dream) then go for it, but for me I will weave it into my everyday life.

I like working with kids, I like working in the mental health sector and I like writing. I don't see why I have to give two up to follow just one. They all help me to become the writer that I am.

To me, living (or at least trying to) a life of boldness is accredited to fear. There's a lot of times when fear has actually encouraged me. Or is the right word not fear but curiosity? Fear comes hand in hand with unknown possibilities. We just have to learn how to handle fear.

I'm trying to live a life that's driven by boldness. Trying to achieve things I've never imagined being possible. And in the process, of course I'll experience things that I may think are way above my strengths, and I expect myself to be scared, but I also know myself, and I know that, when the time comes,

I'll try my best to be brave. And just go for it. Because being courageous is a choice; a rewarding choice.

You've got to do the things that scare you.
That's where you'll grow.

It's okay if you can't identify what your big goal is right now.
Start small.

What inspires you?
What's that thing that you just can't leave alone?

everyday thought

Lord, please keep me inspired so I can inspire others

I can't lose my flame again
    For to lose my flame would be to lose myself

Help me to spread truthful words that will encourage people
I don't want to paint over pretty words without any depth

time and change

Time and change
You don't have a choice with them
They are unavoidable

You should learn how to handle change
You should learn how to manage your time

If you don't, life will leave you behind

courage

I used to be the type of person that waited for great things to happen to me.

I was reluctant to cross the line and reach out for what I wanted.

Part of the reason was because I thought the gift of courage was not for me.

That there was a gene of fearlessness that wasn't passed on to me.

I admired those who made brave decisions so effortlessly.

Subconsciously, I created a false belief that some people were destined to be fearless and others were born to be timid.

Being constantly surrounded by those, let's call them 'gutsy', people in my life created an internal battle. I was surrounded by examples of what I wanted to become but I thought, "We can't all be like that."

There have been things I've wanted to say or do but this little man called fear told me no and I listened.

Let me share a time when I badly wanted to do something, but I was just so darn scared.

It was my last weekend in Sri Lanka with the girls. We hired a catamaran for the day and they provided us with snacks and different activities such as snorkelling and paddle boarding. Now, the thing with me is that I'm not a fan of ocean activities. I'm fine in a swimming pool because I can see the bottom and, if anything, I can quickly hold on to the edge. The lifeguards encouraged everyone to jump off into the water; a part of me was excited and the other part didn't want to die (dramatic, I know). I took pictures as each girl jumped off until I was the last one, but with each girl jumping my stomach got into tighter knots. I was fake smiling and faking excitement because I was trying to stay positive so that I would be able to dive off.

Then it was my turn and I just froze (with my plastic smile). Have you ever believed you could do something, but the moment it comes to it, you freeze?

It was such a conflicting moment for me. I got myself into a state and the idea didn't seem as fun anymore, but I still wanted to do it.

I couldn't physically bring myself to do it and it was very disappointing. I had a moment when I took a deep breath, and was going for it, but then look down into the ocean, I thought, "Nope nope nope," and retreated. It was in that instant I let fear win, and let myself down.

My German friend was the first to get back on the catamaran and, as soon as she got closer, I cried uncontrollably on her shoulders. Another friend told me it was okay, I didn't have to do it if I didn't want to and my reply was, "Yeah that's the thing, I really want to." I don't know if they really understood why I cried. Eventually – with a lot of nudging – I ended up in the water (climbed the ladder down the side), did some snorkelling, and had a fabulous time.

I remember telling my mum when I got home and she laughed because she thought I was exaggerating. Most of you (like my mum) might ask why I let such a small thing upset me that much. Well, the tears were not from being unable to jump off the catamaran, but it was really because I let fear win in a situation where I knew I could have done it. Have you ever looked back and thought to yourself "Aargh, what's wrong with me, why did I back out?"

It's in the past now, an opportunity that I missed but I don't dwell on anymore as I learned something in that moment. I learned to recognise that split moment when bravery and terror are on a balanced scale and only one breath can tip it over to either side. A very pivotal moment.

I actually remembered this moment two years later as I waited to bungee jump off the bridge at Victoria Falls. I told myself "If you start second guessing now, you'll let fear get a foot in. Just take a breath and jump. Don't think about the 'what if'. Be in this moment." And that's exactly what I did.

Whatever it is that you need or want to do, it is important for you to know that nothing is out of your reach. The pleasure of acting despite being fearful is much more satisfying than regret. Oh regret now that's another topic!

I find that these days, when I want to do something and I feel scared, I kind of just do it anyway (knowing that it could either go right or wrong) and as soon as I realise that I'm doing it, I feel very proud of myself. The high I get from knowing that I am capable just drives me. I think it actually increases your self-esteem because it reminds you to believe in yourself. Sometimes I catch myself saying, "Dang, Eve, you did that".

I'm not saying I walk in courage every day – no, absolutely not – but when I do, I flick my braids back and celebrate my success no matter how small.

peace

I used to run with my emotions
Lack of strength to control myself
But you couldn't tell
I kept up appearances
Okay on the outside, shuttered on the inside

Outward appearances can be deceiving
I'm happier now, but I know you can't really tell
This time it's real, I'm in a better place now

I still look the same as before
Actually, no
Better
I've got that glow
That peaceful glow

Overthinking turned into peace
Loneliness turned into peace
Anger turned into peace

I ride on peace these days
It's my portion

What worked for me?

A daily ritual of
Forgiving

Affirmations
Praying

I know what you are thinking
No, it's not that simple
There's a journey to it
It's trying and failing
Being patient
Trying and failing again
Having to find peace daily

But it's also believing that peace is yours
Peace is your portion too
Claim it and fight for it

It's a joint effort
If you seek it, it will find you

Imagine being at a beach
It's too hot and you can hardly breathe
Then that breeze you've been waiting for grazes your face
You surrender to it
You put your hands up and let that breeze touch you everywhere
Leaving you in awe
You instantly forget about the heat and soak in all that fresh
air

Now imagine that feeling when things don't work out
When that application doesn't go through
When you fail that exam

When your marriage starts to become difficult
And you find yourself still standing
Find your breeze in the midst of the heat
That moment when there's chaos but you've found stillness

Find your inner peace daily

God's voice – part 2

"And after the earthquake, a fire but the Lord was not in the fire. And after the fire came a gentle whisper." 1 Kings 19:12 (NIV)

I heard it
I'm sure I did
It's funny because it wasn't what I was expecting
It's funny because I've heard this voice time and time before
I didn't recognise who it was
But it was You
I couldn't work out what your voice sounded like mixed up
    with all the other noises

I feel silly now, getting worked up because I thought I was
    missing out on You
When you were there all along
I can't describe it well enough right now
Still amazed
I'm sure that the next time, I'll understand who it is straight
    away

Today I was stuck in two minds
I've fallen into that trap over and over before
Tired of looking at life through a filter of brokenness
I know it was a filter
Because there was a time when I didn't see life this way

On the floor, I prayed for You to tell me what I needed
My vision blurred with hot tears of pain

Then I heard You clearly say, "I'm there, it's me you'll find."

You spoke so softly
So gently
I could feel your words hugging me

I cried
I felt so relieved, knowing that you've always been there
And you're waiting for me

be the example

Let your gifts shine
Someone is watching you
And you're their last hope

Make them laugh with your humour
Feed them with ambition and belief
Do whatever you can do
Leave better than how you found them

Watch as your story ignites their fire
Tell them how you got through it all
Share your climb to the top
Let them hear your woes
Let them know your defeats
Don't hide your scars from them

Be an example to others
Who we are is worth sharing
Don't think that what you do isn't important

Don't talk yourself out of it
You need to show up, so they can too
You have something that society needs from you
Be the first to open that door

Let your gifts shine
You're here to be the light

be inclusive

I want to be the person that notices others

To be attentive

We live in a place where people fail to notice signs of someone struggling
It's so easy for people to fall through the cracks when no one is paying attention

The world can be a harsh place
So don't add on to other people's pain
Don't be cruel

Be inclusive
Be intentional on focusing on those who need help
Make them a priority
And be the one to make the first conversation

You don't know who you might end up saving

travel

To be honest, growing up I never thought I would visit as many countries as I've been to at my ripe age of twenty-three.

I was born in a place where travelling was for dreamers.

I never noticed or felt left out for not being able to travel because I was young and it wasn't something that was common for me.

In my teenage years, I became infatuated with other cultures.

I wanted to see so many places.

My passport gave me that freedom.

Seeing the wonders of the world.

Knowing that a new adventure waits for me whenever I'm ready.

Leaving home to make another place home.

Having to rely on myself while I'm away.

I'm better abroad than I am at home.

As in, mentally.

I'm less selfish.

I'm more aware.

More generous.

More comfortable.

Travelling made me realise how small I am in the grand scheme of things.

It's the humbling experiences.

Endless numbers of embarrassing stories.

Great conversations with people I will never meet again.
The list goes on…

I spent my money travelling instead of doing my Masters
or saving up for a mortgage.
And people made me feel bad about my decisions.
Apparently, they were not wise choices.

But they were worth it.

What's on your bucket list?

I don't exactly have a bucket list (and I'm not going to force you to make one). But if I did have one, publishing a book would definitely be on it, and now I can tick it off the list (that's not really there haha).

Most people have travelling, skydiving or a hot air balloon experience, which are all incredible things to tick off. But you can also include things such as running a business, learning a new language or conquering your fears.

So, what's on your bucket list?

desert

Hear this.

My friend Mollie and I had about nine days left in our trip to Chile. We only had enough money to either go south to Patagonia, or north to San Pedro. Patagonia was adding up to be too expensive for us at that time.

San Pedro it was.

When me and Mollie are left to do our own planning, we sort of go with the wind.

We booked our flights only and decided to see what would happen next when we got there.

The next day we took a cheap domestic flight to Atacama, San Pedro.

When I say Atacama is a desert, it's a *DESERT* desert.

From the airport, we took an Uber to the coach station that would take us to the town, Atacama.

We fell asleep on the coach, and the coach conductor closed our blinds for us. After a long and HOT coach ride, the conductor woke me up and said, "San Pedro, Atacama ten minutes". I pulled back the blinds and, I kid you not, all I could see was desert, just soil everywhere.

I said to myself, "Nah, this can't be it."

True to what he said, the coach stopped and all those who were on board for San Pedro, Atacama stood up to get off. I woke Mollie up and said, "We're here." I then pulled the blinds open.

We had a moment when we just looked at each other. We didn't say anything, but I knew she was freaking out just like I was deep down.

Everyone told us it was a desert, but we didn't think it was a *desert* desert, you know.

The coach station was literally a medium-sized hut with coach times written on a blackboard, a few chairs and a mini souvenir shop.

I was gobsmacked.

What were we thinking?

Mollie got out her phone to check for Ubers and, no surprise, they were none available.

So, I went to ask for directions to get a taxi from a lady that was sat near the black boards.

Me, in my most Spanish accent, said to her, "Donde Taxi?"

She only replied, "Afuera," and pointed up ahead of me. Guys, I kid you not, all I could see was desert.

I wanted to cry.

We literally stood at the side of the road. Trying to figure out what to do next.

This *hombre* (man), no lie, who had a toothpick in his mouth, came up to us and asked if we wanted a taxi to town.

We literally had no other options. He then gave us a high price and we tried to haggle but he wasn't giving in. So, we pretend to walk away, dragging our suitcases to nowhere (haha, we're so dramatic). He gave in and agreed to the price that we offered.

We got in his truck – one of those that fit three people at the front and an open space at the back for luggage – and drove off.

I literally felt like I was in a Wild West movie.

We sat in silence; he couldn't speak English and we didn't know Spanish.

But I was following the blue dot on my phone maps to see if he was going to the location we gave him.

Now, we hadn't actually booked a place to stay; we just had a list of places we were going to check for room availability.

Looking back now, wow.

If my mum knew, she would never let me out of her sight again.

Do you have any crazy travel stories?

Activity
Satisfaction

Travelling makes me feel so satisfied. Leaving home to chase an adventure is always uplifting for me. Another thing that makes me satisfied is finishing something I've started. Completing this project really made me feel accomplished. It wasn't easy, but it showed me that I'm capable of anything if I put my mind to it.

What leaves you feeling satisfied?

Here is a list of things that people have told me makes them feel more satisfied with themselves:

- **Exercising.** Hitting a new personal best and seeing their physical health improve.
- **Volunteering/helping people.** What's better than offering your time to others?
- **Travelling.** Whether you're gallivanting in your own city or going abroad, new adventures are always liberating.
- **Eating healthy.** I always feel better when I'm eating healthily, and actually stick to it. It makes me feel in control.
- **Reading the Bible/spiritual book.** I find that connecting to a higher being brings me peace and I feel more satisfied with how to live my life; it gives me a sense of direction.
- **Cooking from scratch.** Making a good homemade meal and having everyone ask for more

- **Cleaning/tidying up.** I can have a very unproductive day but if I clean up even for an hour, I somehow get a sense of accomplishment and feel more relaxed.
- **Singing in public/performing.** Showcase your talents. Own the spotlight.
- **Making a friend smile.** People always remember how you made them feel.

Here are some other suggestions:

- Helping the homeless
- Maintaining an active social life
- Doing something new
- Games/completing a puzzle
- Dancing
- Being productive
- Succeeding at something difficult
- Worshipping
- Being efficient with food and time
- Repairing things
- Being creative
- Driving
- DIY
- Forgiving others
- Learning a new language/skill

The list goes on…
Why don't you try something new from the list above?

all that is you

Please be yourself
I promise you
Everything will be okay

And it's going to seem weird at first
And sometimes you'll feel like being yourself isn't the best self
to be

The version that you're embarrassed of

But please be yourself
Embrace all that that is you

Especially when you feel like you're not good enough

You keep wishing to be different
But you are different
And I know this isn't the version of yourself that you want
And you don't fully know how to be yourself
Don't worry; the unreal version of you will fade away with
time

But who you are is what you have
So embrace all that is you

I'm so proud of you

I know you are scared
I know you are clueless about what's going to happen next
But I know that you have big dreams
And you're not ready to settle for less

I know that you have visions that are bigger than where
you currently are
And you are doing everything that you can to make sure
that you make it on the other side

I'm so proud that you're doing this
I'm so proud that you're taking a chance on yourself
I'm so proud that you are stepping into the unknown

I'm so proud of how far you've come

I know that you don't think much of yourself
And you are aware of the competition
You're aware of your limits

But you carry on
You continue to move forwards
You are driven to succeed

I'm celebrating because you gave it your best

I'm so proud of you

and when you are done

I know you've moved on from that storm

The one that nearly took you out; yes, that one

And I wanted to remind you that there are others who are still drowning back there

Sometimes people forget where they came from
And try to erase their past
Seemingly having amnesia

Yes, your supposed to move on from your past, but don't forget it's what led you to where you are now

It's a part of your history

This is a reminder to not look down on someone who is now learning what you used to learn

Because you know how hard that syllabus can be

And you know that the tests are what made you who you are now

Don't forget that once upon a time you were struggling with those modules too

Don't lose compassion for others

Be understanding

Let them know that if you can overcome it, then they can too

And you know how life is full of surprises

You can find yourself going through the same test down the line again

church

I wouldn't be on this journey if it wasn't for my church.

The last few years at church have really made me who I am today.
Spending more time with God and with myself.
I attended the "There Is More" Hillsong conference in July 2018.
I went there expecting more.
I was all fired up during my time there. The whole conference was just spectacular.

Straight after the conference, I went on a family holiday and returned straight to work when I got back. I was slightly disappointed that nothing special had happened in my life since the conference. However, I did realise that I had lost touch with my creative writing and I felt the urge to start writing again. I found myself reflecting, researching and writing a lot more, but I didn't think too much of it. In that process I didn't realise that, that was the start of forming this book. It wasn't until I went back to my conference notes and read a small point I made on 'stale dreams'. Something clicked, and I told myself, "Eve, we will wake up that old stale dream of yours."

So thank you to Hillsong Church…

For encouraging me to be more faithful.
For encouraging me to be more loving.
For helping me to become closer to Jesus.
For great leaders that inspire me to pursue my dreams.
And for surrounding me with loving, supportive people.

To my readers, find yourself a community.

what I'll leave behind

A story of change
A story of faith

A journey of struggle
A journey of strength

A life of hope
A life of courage

A reminder to enjoy life
A reminder to follow your desires

A challenge, for you, to be an encourager
Even if it's just for one person, who will be able to help the
next

What will you leave behind?

and finally

As we part ways, let me encourage you a little bit more

1) Be genuine
   In who you are and what you do

2) Find a balance
   In everything that you do

3) You. Are. A. Masterpiece.
   It sounds clichéd and overused
   But there's no one out there that's like you
   Don't let their voices tell you who you are

author's note

I've always wanted to be an author
Not to write this type of book
But to write novels
Take myself and my readers to a different place
Somewhere that can make them forget the real world
Just for a while
I actually even started to write a novel
But in the midst of life, I started noting down strong
reflections of things happening in my own world
Taken over by the up and downs of life, the only way to
express myself was to write it down
Regurgitating my feelings and emotions onto a blank page
I unintentionally started to create this book

I did this to help myself
Now I'm sharing this with you, hoping that you, too, will
go and help yourselves
And then help others
Hopefully the cycle will continue

Being creative makes me feel like me
It's when I'm most comfortable
And I hope you too find something that makes you feel
comfortable with yourself

Hope you enjoyed this book
Thank you